Imperfectly Vegan Halloween Style, ImperfectlyVegan™ and SacredBite by Lisa Tremont Ota and SacredBite. All rights reserved.

Disclaimer
The nutrition information contained in ImperfectlyVegan™ Halloween Style is general in nature, and should not be relied upon for specific medical conditions and treatments. If you need specific nutrition advice or services, please contact a reliable health professional to discuss your personal situation. All efforts have been made to assure the accuracy of the information contained in this book as of the date of publication. The author disclaims all liability for any medical outcomes that may occur as a result of applying the methods suggested in this book.

www.sacredexploration.com

IMPERFECTLY VEGAN™

HALLOWEEN STYLE

By Lisa Tremont Ota RD, MPH, MA

with

Reilly Gardine, CPT

&

The ImperfectlyVegan™ Team

Imperfectly Vegan

HALLOWEEN STYLE

is dedicated to

my beloved mummy
Alberta Mae Tremont
(May 12, 1941 - July 29, 2018)

for making all of our holidays as fun and special as possible!
Her handmade costumes, captivating decor, and annual pumpkin carving
parties
remain the inspiration behind my love of
Halloween.

And,
to the animals that endure the most frightening circumstances
for no other purpose than human desire.

TABLE OF CONTENTS

FOREWORD

By Dr. Will Tuttle, Ph.D.

The momentum is building. We are continually learning more about the many beneficial effects of eating vegetables, fruits, and whole grains, and the damaging effects of confining and killing animals for food. This delightful book brings these discoveries to our consciousness as inspiring information about how we can transform our lives and our world, and brings them also to our tables as tried-and-true recipes we can relish. Nourishing our understanding of both the why and the how of vegan living, we can live more healthy and productive lives, and become part of the solution to our pressing challenges, rather than being part of the problem. Personally, I am grateful to intrepid culinary explorers like Lisa who are forging new cuisines and new narratives that respond to our contemporary needs and at the same time show how delicious and satisfying plant-based meals can be. Eating healthy and compassionate meals today means that we are acting to help create a harmonious and sustainable world for those who will inhabit it tomorrow. As I point out in The World Peace Diet, our actions, especially the foods we choose to eat, have far greater ramifications than we typically realize.

When we pay for and eat foods from animals, we act in hurtful ways not only toward the animals, but also toward the people who have to do the grisly work of killing animals all day, as well as to those who go hungry because we are feeding valuable grain to pigs, chickens, cows, and farmed fishes so that we can eat meat, eggs, and dairy products. These unfortunate animals are inefficient converters of grain into animal protein, saturated fat, and cholesterol, and create pollution problems that lead to water depletion, climate destabilization, and species extinction as we cut down forests, overfish the oceans, and contaminate water in order to grow feed for livestock. And then, to compound these problems, eating animal foods is the driving force behind many diseases, such as heart disease, diabetes, arthritis, kidney disease, liver disease, obesity and many forms of cancer. As I discuss in The World Peace Diet, veganism is a journey, not a destination. Wherever you are on your journey is the perfect place to be, and further progress is always possible. While perfection itself as a vegan is unattainable, we can always move further along on the path of caring, respect, and healing, both in relation to ourselves, as well as to animals and the other people in our lives. Doing the best we can to reduce and eliminate actions, thoughts, and words that are abusive to animals, ecosystems, and others from the acculturated abuse of our meals.

Physical health, psychological health, spiritual health, cultural health, and ecological health are all interconnected. We are all raised in a culture that mandates meals that are damaging to all these dimensions of health, as well as to our happiness. Questioning the harmful narratives of our culture—like the protein story, the calcium story, and the human superiority story—we can embark on an empowering and fascinating adventure of self-discovery, and help free ourselves and other people, and to cultivate awareness and kindness, is a sure way to increase happiness, peace, and freedom in our world and in ourselves. Veganism is another word for abundance, liberation, and harmony, and while we can never force others to change or to awaken, as we ourselves awaken and light our inner candle, we naturally plant seeds that encourage others to do the same.

There is an abundance of health, beauty, fun, and practical know-how in this book that you hold in your hands. I encourage you to dive in, learn, and give the recipes a whirl, and partake not just of these tasty and creative culinary realities, but of the optimism and caring that underlie them. As the author says: ImperfectlyVegan™. As we each do the best we can, in this moment, we become part of the solution. As we do, the food (and our lives) are getting better. Thank you for reading, questioning, experimenting, and sharing the understanding conveyed in these pages. You help yourself and all of us. We are all connected.

Dr. Will Tuttle

Dr. Will Tuttle, author of the best-selling The World Peace Diet, composer, pianist, and former Zen monk, is co-founder of Karuna Music & Art and the Worldwide Prayer Circle for Animals.

Dr. Tuttle's favorite thing about Halloween: Carving happy pumpkin faces and eating pumpkin pie!

ACKNOWLEDMENTS

After writing The Sacred Art of Eating, it was time to expand upon the invitation to be ImperfectlyVegan™. Wanting assistance and companionship for the process, I wisely approached UC Berkeley's Undergraduate Nutrition Program. Having been a graduate from the school myself, I knew that the students would be enthusiastic, open-minded, and equipped with a solid understanding of nutrition principles. While I had hoped to receive one or two responses, I had instead received an abundance! I couldn't imagine turning anyone away who wanted to be a part of the movement, and so formed The ImperfectlyVegan™ Team. Between their demanding academic schedules and wide variety of outside commitments (many of them studying abroad from locations spanning the planet), they eagerly offered up help whenever and however they could. Activities included recipe development, creating social media posts, writing press releases, designing and implementing Halloween parties, editing, finding research articles, promoting whole food supplementation and, of course, contributing ideas on how to reach various populations with our message. And so, it is with deep gratitude that I present the original ImperfectlyVegan™ Team members: Lucy Wu, Michaela Iglesia, Leandra Padayachee, Sofia Fabbrizio, Chrixy Lam, Eunice Kang, Adeline Wong, Ashley Noronha, Benedicta Jovita, Judy Shan, Kithumini Jayasiri, Wafa Mehboob, Hannah Hanzhi Tong, Katharine Nusbaum, Kanami Kitagawa, Eileen Wu and, especially, Reilly Gardine who has been so tremendously helpful that co-authorship on this particular book was most well-deserved. Indeed, the team has developed much more than featured in this version, so stay tuned for future editions of ImperfectlyVegan™.

Deep appreciation, also, to Patricia and David Koot (Chef and Executive Director, respectively, of SF Wellness Central) for their weekly offering of a delicious vegan dinner along with informative education, in which they have honored me multiple times as their speaker; Dr. Will Tuttle (Author of The World Peace Diet) and Ray Cooper (Founder of VegCurious) for honoring me with their sincere support for the intention behind ImperfectlyVegan™ and of my related activities; Marcus Mebes and Paul Savage for making content come alive through their creative design work; Chris Winsey, for holding the vision and moving things forward when this book was the last thing that I could think about; and Eric and Matthew, for their patience and guidance with all the techie stuff!

WHY IMPERFECTLY VEGAN™?

Given our knowledge about the way food can transform our health and lives, what is the diet that best helps us thrive?

The benefits of a plant based diet are well documented, though there are complexities and challenges involved in obtaining the health advantages of a meat free diet. Because vegans comprise a small percentage of the population, it is challenging to conclude much about their disease rates, though there is mounting research due to the increase in the popularity of the diet. However, vegetarian and vegan categories combined have been found to have a significantly lower mortality rate than non-vegetarian ones. In other words, their practitioners live longer.

Heart Disease and Cancer

Heart disease and cancer are the two leading causes of death, but both of them are preventable. According to a systematic review from 2017, vegans have the lowest incidence of cancer when compared to vegetarians and omnivores. The same study showed a 25% decrease in incidence of heart disease on a meat-free diet.

Epigenetics

We now know that we can live significantly longer with better health. The advancing field of epigenetics ("above genetics") helps us recognize that we are not necessarily set up to experience the same outcomes as our ancestors, despite our similar genes. Epigenetics studies the factors—including diet, exercise, exposure to toxins, and even our attitude—that impact gene expression. It also considers the electromagnetic impact of quantum physics, which helps explain the "placebo effect" in which people's health improves simply because they think they have taken a medicine that will bring healing, when in fact they have not.

As Richard Rudd, developer of the Gene Keys, a guide to unlocking the higher purpose hidden in our DNA, says, "What all of this means is that you can never be a victim of your DNA. Neither can you be a victim of fate. You can only be a victim of your attitude. Every though you think, every feeling you have, every word you utter, and every action you take directly programs your genes and therefore your reality."

Whether or not you experience the same poor health outcomes as your grandparents depends much more on your lifestyle practices than on the fact that you share the same genes. This concept is most visible when we consider that a true genetic mutation generally occurs over multiple generations, yet chronic diseases are increasing at a rate that an increased number of people with a gene for those particular disease states cannot substantiate. This pattern indicates that something beyond genetics is at play, and those factors, especially diet, are largely within our control. You are not your mother's genes!

"If we don't pull our act together soon, this generation of children will have shorter life spans than their parents."
Dr. David Katz

Overweight and Obesity

According to the Centers for Disease Control's (CDC's) 1999–2014 National Health and Nutrition Examination Survey, more than two out of three American adults are overweight or obese. Again, we are constantly transforming, and the direction in which we transform is dependent primarily upon what we eat. If we eat poorly, we will transform toward poor health. If we eat optimally, we will transform toward optimal health. As one example, my father underwent double-bypass surgery at an early age. But because he radically changed the way he eats, he has far surpassed the odds and just turned eighty (2018). Our cells turn over constantly. Change how you nourish your body, and change your life for good!

One of the primary reasons a plant-based lifestyle is so effective at reducing the risk of these diseases is that it helps people maintain a healthy weight. Lower body weight is associated with reduced mortality (death) and morbidity (illness) across the lifespan. Consistent evidence from clinical trials shows that vegetarian diets reduce body weight, and that vegans tend to weigh the least. Population-based studies have shown that body weight, or body mass index (BMI), is lower for vegetarians than for non-vegetarians, and that the caloric intake of a vegetarian diet can be as many as 460 calories lower than that of non-vegetarians. It's hard to eat too much when you're filling up on plant foods!

Being ImperfectlyVegan™ is a sound strategy for losing weight, keeping it off for good, and enjoying the health benefits! In addition to living longer, vegetarians also age more healthfully -- with advantages such as better age-related cognitive (brain) function, reduced cataracts, and reduced diverticular disease -- and experience physical benefits like healthy, glowing skin and increased energy.

If you are overweight, even modest weight loss can help you improve cholesterol levels, reduce triglyceride levels, lower blood pressure, lower blood glucose (sugar) levels, and significantly reduce your risk of developing diabetes, all of which are risk factors for heart disease. In regard to cancer, researchers report that as many as ninety thousand cancer deaths could be prevented each year if Americans maintained a healthy weight.

All Cancers

Furthermore, a plant-based diet can reduce our risk of all cancers combined, especially gastrointestinal cancer, cancer of the female organs (including breast, ovarian, uterine, and cervical), and possibly respiratory cancer, because of the highly beneficial compounds found in plants. Evidence suggests, for example, that dietary phytochemicals (beneficial plant compounds), such as genistein, and other isoflavones from soy products; epigallocatechin-3-gallate and other polyphenols in tea; and isothiocyanates and indole-3-carbinol from cruciferous vegetables are likely to alter a person's susceptibility to cancer.

Needless to say, prevention is the way to go. Unfortunately, the medical system focuses more energy on treating symptoms than treating causes. When it comes to chronic disease, medical intervention is often a short sighted approach that harms more than it heals. The unhealthy cells underlying our diseases are constantly transforming.

Provided with an optimal plant-based diet, they may regenerate, recover, and become revitalized.

Positive Affect on Other Conditions

Remember that "disease" is just a word that is used to refer to unhealthy cells in the body. The same issues underlie most diseases. So, in addition to helping to prevent or reverse heart disease and cancer, a plant-based diet may also facilitate the healing of many conditions. Though the research varies as to a how plant-based diet affects these conditions, nevertheless a positive correlation of benefit is cited for asthma, allergies, and sinus infections; skin disorders, such as acne; endometriosis and infertility; migraines; depression and other psychological disorders; heartburn; arthritis; joint pain; diabetes; attention deficit hyperactivity disorder (ADHD); thyroid dysfunction; Lyme disease; chronic fatigue syndrome; autoimmune disorders, such as fibromyalgia and lupus; leaky-gut syndrome; and gastrointestinal disorders, such as Crohn's disease, irritable bowel syndrome (IBS), celiac disease, diverticulitis, and ulcerative colitis.

"WE ALL have a unique, lifelong relationship with food. But for too many of us, that relationship is broken. We are born into amazing human bodies on a planet that serves up a bounty of delicious and nutritious foods, yet our disconnect with our bodies and with the earth has led us into a global food frenzy. Food can energize us and create optimal health and longevity, but it can also drain us and the planet, and lead us toward premature death and devastation." - Lisa Tremont Ota: The Sacred Art of Eating

The body is wise beyond our understanding. It is our job to feed it well so that it can best do its job in helping us to live a full and healthy life!

Humanitarian Values

In addition to health, the decision to be ImperfectlyVegan™ can be based on other important values as well, such as limiting cruelty to animals and preserving the planet. Beloved author and activist Alice Walker says, "Animals of the world exist for their own reasons. They were not made for humans any more than blacks were made for whites or women for men."

Being ImperfectlyVegan™ is about making a commitment to all of life. It also allows for a dose of reality. Certainly, increasing numbers of animal rights activists, environmentalists, and health professionals are working toward a vegan world and are thus steadfast in their commitment to a vegan lifestyle. The degree to which someone is ImperfectlyVegan™ depends on their personal level of commitment, experience, and circumstances, all of which may change at different points in time. While the health advantages of a vegetarian diet compared with those of a non vegetarian diet are well documented and highly significant, when it comes to giving up eggs and small amounts of dairy, those differences are not as significant. As such, the reason for abstaining from these foods rests on the cruelty that is inflicted upon the animals providing them, as well as concerns for the environment.

I find that more and more young people are turning to a plant-based diet because of an experience of visiting a slaughterhouse or factory farm. Health isn't much of a concern to them at their age, but witnessing violence against animals makes an impact. Animals raised for food live miserable, hopeless lives. Being ImperfectlyVegan™ also allows you to support the planet, which is in desperate need of our help.

Our Precious Planet

A 2005 study by the University of Chicago found that one person switching from a meat-based diet to a plant-based diet could save about the same amount of carbon dioxide as trading in a Toyota Camry for a Toyota Prius! That's because raising cattle requires about eighty calories of fossil fuel to cultivate one food calorie, whereas only

The Dalai Lama said:

"I have been particularly concerned with the sufferings of chickens for many years. It was the death of a chicken that finally strengthened my resolve to become vegetarian. These days, when I see a row of plucked chickens hanging in a meat shop, it hurts. I find it unacceptable that violence is the basis of some of our food habits."

two calories of fossil fuel are required to cultivate one food calorie of grains, fruits, and vegetables. Furthermore, cattle belch methane, a greenhouse gas that is twenty times more potent than carbon dioxide.

Financially Sound

And—as if we really need another reason—by being green, you'll keep more green in your wallet! While prices vary widely, an average pound of nonorganic factory-farmed ground beef costs around $5 and a pound of chicken breasts $4. A pound of canned beans, in contrast, costs less than $1. The difference is even greater when you purchase high quality, organic, grass fed beef. One couple figured they could save $2,000–3,000 per year by eating a plant-based diet. And, last but certainly not least, being ImperfectlyVegan™ is fun, easy, and delicious!

What Does it Mean to Be Imperfectly Vegan™?

So what exactly is being ImperfectlyVegan™? Well, generally there are four different types of vegetarian diets:

• Vegan: a vegetarian diet that excludes all animal products, such as meat, poultry, fish, eggs, milk, cheese, and other dairy products.

- Lacto-vegetarian: a vegetarian diet that excludes meat, poultry, fish, and eggs but includes dairy products.
- Lacto-ovo-vegetarian: a vegetarian diet that excludes meat, poultry, and fish but includes eggs and dairy products. Most vegetarians in the United States fall into this category.
- Semi Vegetarian or flexitarian: a semi vegetarian diet with a focus on vegetarian food, but involving occasional consumption of meat, poultry, or fish.

And now, introducing a new type of vegetarian lifestyle: ImperfectlyVegan™. I created this term for the following reasons:
- A vegan diet is healthiest for both humans and the earth.
- A traditional vegan diet is too extreme for most people to want to attempt.
- Even some of the most committed vegans will deviate, whether consciously or not.
- Vegetarianism can be vague, but using a term that includes the word "vegan" keeps the focus on a plant-based diet.
- Following a vegan diet most of the time is realistic and provides huge benefits to health, to animals, and to the planet.
- Being ImperfectlyVegan™ is a spiritual path toward increased consciousness and unity of body, mind, and spirit.
- Being ImperfectlyVegan™ is nutritious and delicious!

I first came up with the term "Imperfectly Vegan" in response to people asking me about my lifestyle: "Are you a vegetarian?" Well, not exactly. And then I'd have to explain in which ways I was or wasn't a vegetarian. "Are you a vegan?" That felt close, but I never felt comfortable calling myself a vegan, because there are times when I do consume animal products, both consciously and not. And so I began to respond by saying that I am Imperfectly Vegan. I noticed that people seemed to understand what I meant without my having to explain anything. At more than one event when I have unveiled this term, I have even heard a collective sigh in the room.

ImperfectlyVegan™ piques people's curiosity, and many seem interested in locat-

ing themselves within that definition. It feels doable and represents a clearer step toward plant-based eating than vegetarianism does; it engenders a sense of peace, ease, and hope in people who are interested in following a vegetarian diet but are unsure whether they can successfully do so; and it seems to make sense to those who already practice a vegan lifestyle but admit to consuming small amounts of animal foods from time to time.

Discard All-or-Nothing Thinking

In the field of nutrition, we speak of dietary patterns. There is an important distinction between assessing a person's nutrient intake based on an overall pattern of eating versus just one meal or even a full day of eating. In regard to being ImperfectlyVegan™, this means that it is much more beneficial that someone strive to eat a plant-based diet most of the time, with an occasional turn to animal foods, than to eat an omnivorous diet most of the time, with the occasional absence of flesh. Not to allow for the small inclusion of animal foods would mean that fewer people would attempt a plant-based diet at all.

Would I love to see everyone follow a plant-based diet? Absolutely! But my training and education in public health have made me all too aware of the realities behind such a desire. Thus, offering up the practice of being ImperfectlyVegan™ provides an avenue that more and more people can practice without undue pressure to be absolutist or extremist. As your experience with a plant-based diet grows, you will find that animal products are increasingly less appetizing and satisfying for various reasons.

Imperfectly Vegan™: Halloween Style

TESTIMONIALS

"In a world with harmful social conditioning where confusion is the norm, the ImperfectlyVegan™ idea provides us with a starting place for having conversations on real life issues, as tough as these subjects may be. Food, in my opinion, is the basis of our awakening and nonviolent transformation. ImperfectlyVegan™ is focusing on the bigger picture around food and giving us the opportunity to have honest discussions."

- Robin Housley, activist

Robin's favorite thing about Halloween: Going to Haunted Houses.

"ImperfectlyVegan™ resonates with me. Nobody's perfect, after all. It's not oppressive. It takes the pressure off!"

- Phil Isaia, spiritual teacher

Phil's favorite thing about Halloween: Scaring people!

"ImperfectlyVegan™, for me, is a mindset that I will not become dogmatic in my approach to being vegan. Although I'm vegan for moral and ethical, as well as health, reasons, it's my own path to walk, and if I mistakenly have something that has cheese or milk or honey in it, I won't berate myself for it and I won't chastise the sources of that food, and instead will still thank them for their efforts. It means knowing the difference between having compassion for all life on this planet, regardless of what that life looks like or which animal or plant kingdom we've placed it into.

ImperfectlyVegan™ also helps me avoid using vegan philosophy to pretend I'm better than those who aren't vegan."

- Sean Butman, naturopathic healer

Sean's favorite thing about Halloween: The inspiration to make all sorts of pumpkin pie treats.

"We don't live in a black and white world. There's no such thing as perfection, and not everyone is the same. However, the earthlings of this planet all share in their desire to avoid suffering - whether that be from injury, sickness, or lack of life sustaining resources. While being vegan is certainly not a cure all for the ills of the world, or a means to stop all suffering, it's certainly a start. Though systemic change is what's needed to allow everyone on earth to thrive, being ImperfectlyVegan™ is a step that we are able to make today. It is a step that allows us to care, think critically, and challenge the values of the world we live in. It is a step that gives us permission to try, and also fail, while providing better hope for the future."

- Reilly Gardine, activist

Reilly's favorite thing about Halloween: Adorning the house with skulls and other Halloween themed decorations.

"ImperfectlyVegan™ is a very powerful term to me because it describes how I eat in a way that gives me self-compassion for when I am not perfectly vegan. So when I have a bit of goat cheese on my salad or a bite of a quiche, I still feel that I am being congruent with my description of being ImperfectlyVegan™."

- StaciJoy Ellis, holistic nurse

StaciJoy's favorite thing about Halloween: Seeing the innocence and excitement in the faces of children when they dress up in costume.

THE HISTORY OF HALLOWEEN

The history of Halloween begins about 2,000 years ago with the ancient Celtic pagan festival of Samhain, or feast of "summer's end." This holiday took place October 31st through November 1st, celebrating the new year and the end of the harvest season. It was seen as a liminal time, where the boundaries of the world of the living and the world of the dead were blurred.

People would light bonfires and perform rituals, while wearing costumes to ward off ghosts and evil spirits. Treats were offered to appease the souls of the dead who were thought to cross into the world at this time. Places were set at the dinner table, and offerings of food and drink, or portions of the crop, were left outside. It was believed that these gifts would please the spirits and ensure the people and their farmed animals would survive the winter. Household festivities served as divinations for the future, especially regarding death and marriage. Apples and hazelnuts were often used in these festivities, as apples were associated with immortality in Celtic mythology, and hazelnuts were associated with divine wisdom.

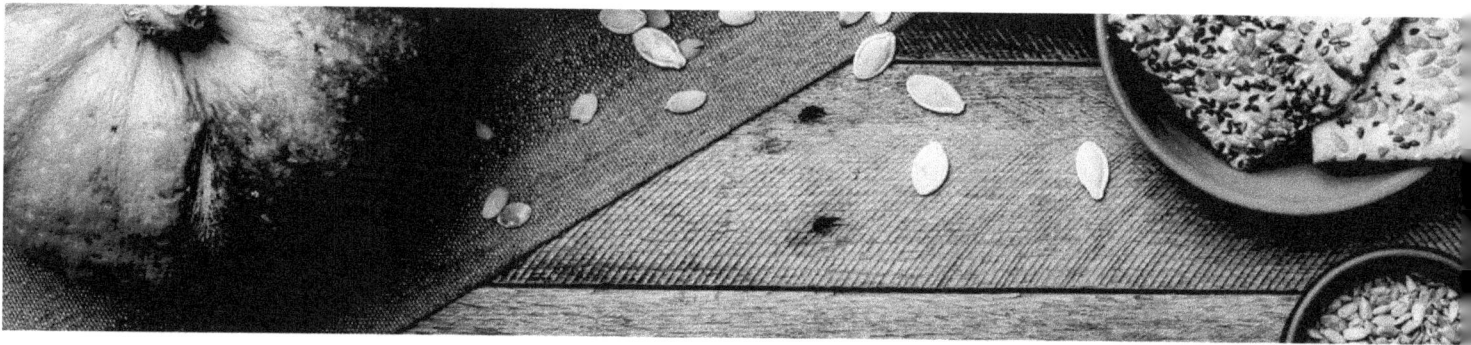

Later, after Christianity had spread to Celtic lands, November 1st became the Feast for All Saints, where "soul cakes" would be made to remove or placate fearful ghosts from peoples' homes. To indicate that these cakes were alms, they were often marked with a cross. In order to honor the dead, All Souls' Day was developed alongside All Saints Day, occuring a day later. October 31st became the Eve of All Saints, or All Hallows' Eve. On this day during the medieval period, groups of poor people and children would go "souling," traveling door to door to collect these "soul cakes." They were given in exchange for prayers honoring the person answering the door's deceased relatives and friends. This practice is sometimes seen as the precursor to modern day "trick-or-treating." While souling, some would carry hollowed out and carved turnips with them, representing the souls of the dead. Immigrants to North America would later use the native pumpkin, which was much easier to carve and would become the characteristic jack-o-lantern. The tradition of dressing in costume and going trick-or-treating may have also come from "mumming" and "guising," in which people would disguise themselves and ask for food at peoples' doors.

In the 19th century, as Irish immigrants traveled to the United States, they brought with them their Halloween customs and traditions. Borrowing from the Irish and English, Americans would dress up in costume and go door to door asking for treats or money. Apple bobbing, or using only your teeth to retrieve an apple from a large tub of water, was another common activity of the Irish and English. People also did tricks with apple peels, hazelnuts, yarn, and mirrors to predict the name or face of their future spouse. In the late 1800s, there was a move in the U.S. to make the holiday more about community, and less about pranks, ghosts, and witchcraft.

Parties centered around food, festive costumes, and games became more of norm, and the superstitions and religious aspects of the holiday started dwindling. What we know now as trick-or-treating did not start in the U.S. until after the Great Depression, as a way to curtail Halloween mischief that had gotten out of hand. It was a positive, community-based activity, and was encouraged over the holiday's characteristic pranks and vandalism. It took a short break during World War II, because of sugar rationing, but resumed during the postwar baby boom. Candy companies, no longer constrained by a sugar shortage, began capitalizing on the lucrative ritual. These companies carried out big marketing campaigns to advertise for the holiday, which was growing alongside suburbanization. Today Americans spend more than $6 million each year on Halloween, making it the second largest commercial holiday in the nation.

As we can see, this holiday has transformed throughout time, both in meaning and in practice. Its long and unfixed history gives us another clue as to the state of the universe - it's always changing! Water serves as another remarkable symbol of this transformation. Consider that just two molecules, hydrogen and oxygen, can restructure themselves over and over into different states: liquid, vapor, and solid. And, as with oxygen, we cannot live without it—it is essential to almost every physiological reaction in the body. As such, it is imperative that we drink water regularly if we want to give our bodies the best chance possible to experience optimal health.

Our universe is not static, and therefore we should not be either. Let's draw inspiration from one of the most transformative holidays to transform our health!

SCARY STATS

• Almost every child over 10 in developed countries has fatty streaks (precursors to plaque) in their arteries (Robbins Basic Pathology)

• 1 in 6 dairy cows in the US suffers from clinical mastitis (a painful infection in the udders which impacts the quality of their milk) (USDA)

• There are over 450 drugs or feed additives used in the animal agriculture industry (FDA)

• Approximately 80% of all antibiotics in the US are given to farmed animals (FDA)

• Livestock covers 45% of the Earth's surface (International Livestock Research Institute)

• The livestock sector contributes more greenhouse gas emissions than all transportation combined (FAO)

• 64% of the world is expected to experience water shortages by 2025 (FAO)

• 7 million pounds of excrement (poop!) are produced every minute by animals raised for food in the US (USDA)

• More than 35% of Americans are classified as obese (CDC)

• 88% of pork chops, 90% of ground beef, and 95% of chicken breasts sampled from grocery stores contained fecal bacteria (FDA)

• $2.7 trillion dollars was spent on healthcare in the US in 2014, an increase from $1.2 trillion in 2000 (CDC)

Imperfectly Vegan™: Halloween Style

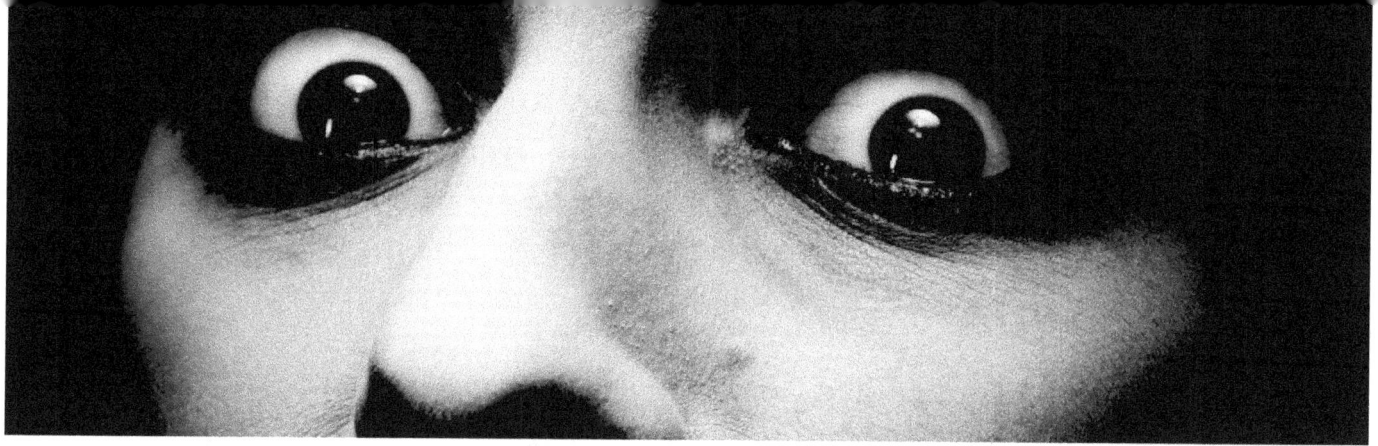

A HORROR FILM COME TO LIFE

Warning: Reality can be scarier than fiction. Some graphic content to follow.

The Nightmarish Treatment of Animals

Go into an animal agriculture facility today, and you may just well think you've entered into a nightmare! Animal food operations are not the idyllic meadow pasture with little red barn scenes that many have in their minds when they think of animal farming. Instead, animals raised for food are subject to filthy and uninhabitable living conditions, abuse, starvation, cannibalism, and more!

Egg-Laying Hens

Some of the arguably worst treated in animal agriculture are egg laying hens. They are crammed into tiny cages, stacked one on top of the other, in a large shed that reeks of ammonia. If they are hens from a "cage-free" farm, they are packed into large warehouses where they technically have access to a door that leads to an outside area, but often are never able to access it because of the intensive crowding. In both of these conditions, it's common to see what could only be described as a horror scene - half dead hens getting trampled on by larger hens, mutilated and rotting flesh, oozing eye infections, cannibalism of weaker hens by stronger ones, and birds covered in feces, unable to move. If it's a caged facility, hens' feet will often become deformed by the wire cages, or even fuse with them! Birds are forced to live in cages on top of, or under, dead ones, with no escape possible. However, the male chicks born in this industry don't even stand a chance -- they are ground up alive in a macerator, gassed to death, or left to suffocate and die in large waste bins. The over 200 million that suffer this fate don't produce eggs, so they're seen as no more than disposable objects.

Commercial Chicken Farming

The chickens raised for their flesh don't fare too much better. 9 billion of these animals are killed on U.S. farms every year, meaning 24 million per day, 17,000 each minute, or 285 every second. Chilling, isn't it? Like chickens raised for their eggs, they are crammed into warehouses with tens, if not hundreds of thousands, of other individuals, so tightly packed it's hard to move. The uric acid in the constant layer of excrement on the floor causes burns and ulcerations to their feet and bodies. From the inside out they suffer, too. Broilers, as they're called, have been selectively bred to grow three times faster than they would normally, causing muscle mass to develop far faster than the rest of their body. This leads to deformation, broken bones, respiratory disorders, and heart failure. These birds are also routinely pumped with antibiotics, which help them grow even faster. When it's time to go to slaughter, chickens are snatched up and stuffed into trucks, often having their bones broken in the process. Once at the slaughterhouse, they are shocked by an electric water bath designed to stun them before their throat is slit by an automated blade. Hopefully, they bleed to death at this point. But if not, they are boiled alive in a scalding tank meant to remove their feathers. This is the end for these chickens, who have lived their short six week life in constant misery.

Cows and Beef - Another Nightmare

As for cows raised for their meat, the nightmare continues. Since they, like all animals raised for food, are viewed as mere commodities, cows who grow the fastest and largest are the most valued. Thus, cows are selectively bred, with the largest males chosen as breeders, and the rest castrated without anesthetics or pain relief.

Male calves also have their horns cut or burned off, an intensely painful process. The next step of mutilation is branding, where an extremely hot or cold iron is pressed into their skin until they bear a permanent flesh wound that designates identification and ownership. For the next 6-8 months of their life, they are grazed on grassy pastures, with no protection from extreme weather. Floods, scorching heat, hypothermic conditions, and wild predators all pose threats to their wellbeing and safety. After this grazing period, cows are sent to confined feedlots where they are fed a grain based diet meant to put large amounts of weight on them in a very short time. This food is not natural for cows, and can cause huge buildups of gas or even stomach acid, causing a painful condition called acute acidosis. Most of the animals in these CAFOs (confined animal feeding operations) are also given growth hormones and antibiotics, with the purpose of making them grow even larger. At only 12-14 months old, the cows are loaded onto trucks. Here they will spend up to 36 stressful hours deprived of food and water, often forced to stand in their own vomit and diarrhea. Once at the slaughterhouse, cows are supposed to be stunned with a captive bolt pistol that drives a metal rod through the skull and into the brain to induce unconsciousness. This step is not always followed, and it's not uncommon for animals to be shackled by their feet and slit by the throat while fully conscious. They are then skinned and dismembered, sometimes while still kicking and screaming.

Dairy Cows Suffering

Dairy cows suffer the same fate as cows raised for their flesh -- they are sent to the slaughterhouse and turned into ground beef. However, before they're sent to slaughter, they endure a life even more horrific than those raised specifically for their meat. Since mammals don't produce milk unless they are expecting a baby, cows are repeatedly impregnated every year. This is often done by strapping a female cow to a rack (which has historically been referred to in the industry as a "rape rack") and artificially inseminating her. After forty weeks, she births a calf who is taken from her a few days later, at most, so that her milk can be used for human consumption. This is severely distressing, and it's not unheard of for mother cows to bellow and pace for days, grieving the loss of their children. If this calf is female, she will become a dairy cow like her mom. If the calf is male, unless he's saved for breeding, he will be sent to auction and slaughtered after a few days or months. Often he will be raised as a veal calf, subjected to extreme confinement and starvation for 16-18 weeks before he is killed for his flesh. Mother cows experience this same cycle multiple times throughout their life, meanwhile enduring two to three daily automatic milkings by a machine. This is a stressful process meant to extract the most milk possible, and it's not uncommon for cows to develop mastitis. This is a painful swelling of mammary tissues often induced by trauma from these machines, in which pathogenic (disease causing) bacteria enter through openings in her teat, leading to infection, inflammation, and abnormal milk. Cows also suffer from lameness, injury, sickness, or end up collapsing from the exhaustion on their bodies. For this reason they are sent to slaughter at only five years old, too weak to continue the process. Cows naturally live over twenty years.

Pigs in Misery

Another animal that suffers immensely is the pig. Raised for ham, bacon, and sausage, pigs are viewed as money making objects, and are treated only as such. Born into farrowing crates so small mother pigs can't turn around, but have to lay on their sides to feed their piglets, pigs make a depressing entrance into the world. Their tails are docked so as to avoid serious damage when they inevitably bite each other as stressful conditions and hunger lead to aggression. Males are routinely castrated without anesthetic, and some females become destined to become mother pigs themselves. These sows will languish in intensive confinement, where loneliness and deprivation often cause these animals to go visibly insane. Their misery will only end when they are finally slaughtered only a few years later because their bodies are so spent. For pigs that are simply raised for food, they endure a lifetime of extreme crowding, poor ventilation, and rampant illness. The floors are covered in feces, the air is so bad most pigs end up with pneumonia, and corpses become scattered amongst the living. They never get to see the sun, and their feet never touch anything but a bare, hard floor. The most unlucky are eaten alive by other pigs. Fed growth hormones and antibiotics, pigs grow at an alarmingly fast pace, and are ready to be shipped in transport trucks at about six months old. Around a million of these pigs will die just in transport. Once at the slaughterhouse, which typically kills about a thousand animals per hour, pigs are stunned and then boiled. Due to improper stunning, many pigs are scalded alive, squealing in pain and fear the entire time.

Human Suffering

The workers at all these plants suffer, too, and it's important to remember the human rights violations that occur at virtually every factory farm and slaughterhouse. Most of these workers are not at this job by choice, but rather by necessity. They perform the work out of desperation to feed their families, or fear of deportation. Many of these workers are undocumented, which means they aren't granted the protections legally required for employees, and can't safely unionize or fight back to protect themselves without risk of expulsion from the country. Most can't even legally organize without being spied on, harassed, threatened, or fired, even though they are supposed to have the right of freedom of association. Human rights violations are rampant, with extraordinarily high rates of injury on the job. An injury in these facilities could mean dismissal, leaving the worker without a job and without any compensation. This is why injuries often go unreported, not that everyone could afford to do anything about their injuries anyways, as many have no health insurance. The government laws, policies, regulations, and enforcement that do exist are insufficient to protect the health and safety of these workers.

CDC Stats on Agri-Workers

According to the CDC, "Every day, about 167 agricultural workers suffer a lost-work-time injury. Five percent of these injuries result in permanent impairment." The air quality is so bad that respiratory illness is common in more than half of these workers, who breathe in ammonia and hydrogen sulfide on a daily basis. The CDC also found that in 2012, there were 20.2 deaths per 100,000, making this deadly work. Even for those that survive the perils of the job, slaughterhouse work has been linked to PTSD (Post Traumatic Stress Disorder) and PITS (Perpetration-Induced Traumatic Stress), in addition to other trauma induced manifestations such as an increase in incidence of alcohol and drug abuse, crime rates, and domestic abuse. This makes sense, as these workers are subjected to, and forced to participate in, extremely violent, graphic, and emotionally disturbing actions over and over again. They essentially have to live in and be a part of a horror film every day.

NOW...
Let's explore how the fun, food, and activities of Halloween can nourish positive TRANSFORMATION!

FUN HALLOWEEN ACTIVITIES

VISITING A PUMPKIN PATCH is a favorite activity for all ages! Like us, pumpkins come in all shapes, colors, and sizes, and make different contributions. Types of pumpkins include Cinderella, Jack-o-lantern (a market term for pumpkins that are grown with large cavities and thin walls suitable for carving), Japanese (also called kabocha), Mini (used primarily for decor), and Pie (having a high flesh-to-seed ratio). With so many options to choose from, the search for just the right one can be a fun adventure. During this time of year, this fruit reminds us of the divine's ability to transform our lives. Full of fiber and beta-carotene, pumpkins provide us with an abundance of good nutrition that will help transform our bodies in a positive direction. Many pumpkin patches also offer train rides, haystack tunnels, corn mazes, bean bag toss games, pony rides, and more!

This year, try HOSTING A HEALTHY HALLOWEEN PARTY. It doesn't have to be boring! In fact, using the guidelines below, it will be especially captivating! Part of the transformation process involves changing how we view and relate to food, especially during the holidays. Halloween doesn't necessarily entail candy and sugar covered treats, and healthy doesn't have to mean bland and uninspired. You can still create a Halloween themed party that spooks, but leaves the scary out of the ingredients. And, interestingly, because many Western Christian denominations encourage, although no longer require, abstinence from meat on All Hallows' Eve, the tradition of eating certain vegetarian foods for this vigil developed. Such foods include apples, colcannon (a traditional Irish vegetarian dish of mashed potatoes with kale or cabbage), cider, potato pancakes and soul cakes. Some of these dishes use butter and milk, but can easily be made vegan.

"Drop on In for a Tasty Bite!"
(said the spider to the fly)

This October, host a Halloween Brunch that offers thrills, chills, and good nutrition! Here's a tasty menu that's sure to both fright and delight:

• BOOgels and SCREAM Cheese
• SPOOKY Cookies
• NOT-DEAD Bread (100% whole grain bread)
• Fruit Salad with BOOberries, BOOnanas, and CADAVERloupe
• PUMPKIN Muffins (recipe below)
• PUMPKIN Pie Pancakes (recipe below)

Beverages might include:

• Hot Apple SPIDER
• DECAPITATED Coffee
• GREEN WITCH Tea
• EYEBALL Punch (recipe below)
• PUMPKIN Smoothies

Your GOBLINS and GHOULS are sure to enjoy these tasty bites!

This Halloween Brunch was an example of transformation in and of itself. Eighteen years ago, when my two sons were ages four and one, it just so happened that I was scheduled to host our local playgroup on the week of Halloween. I prepared all the usual items that kids and moms like to eat and drink. But, the night before the event, something happened! Suddenly, the bagels and cream cheese morphed into BOOgels and SCREAM cheese. The hot apple cider became hot apple SPIDER. The cantaloupe grew into CADAVERloupe, and so on... I had so much fun with the idea that I created signs to place with the foods so that everyone (well, the moms at least) could have a chuckle or two. Over the years, I continued to expand upon the theme. And, as my relationship with food transformed to being ImperfectlyVegan™, the foods transformed, too. I share this idea with you as a way to introduce your friends and family to new vegan foods while having lots of fun, too! Feel free to copy the signs and mimic the invitation. As conveyed in Chapter One of The Sacred Art of Eating, I feel very strongly about the concept of THE INVITATION! Indeed, the best I can do is extend an invitation for you to be ImperfectlyVegan™. And the best you can do is to extend that same invitation to others. We cannot force anyone to eat vegan any more than we can force a baby to eat when it doesn't want to do so. So, please... ENJOY! And feel free to share your own transformations on our ImperfectlyVegan™ Facebook Group. Resources for your healthy Halloween party can be found in the Appendix and include the following:

- Party Preparations List
- Instructions to make entertaining signs for your transformed menu items
- Puzzle sheets

PUMPKIN CARVING

One of the most entertaining examples of a pumpkin's transformative qualities comes when we turn this fruit into a JACK-O-LANTERN. When we place a candle inside, it lights up even the darkest night. This was a favorite activity for 'All Hallows' Day, dedicated to remembering the dead. After the interior is opened up and hallowed out, the exterior provides an open canvas of artistic creativity. Once completed, the outside has metamorphosed into something new, while still resembling its original form of a pumpkin. Nowadays, the squash's exterior is often painted, allowing for even more creative options. Though originally done with turnips, the shift to pumpkins in North America highlights the transformative value of this fun activity. The jack-o-lantern shows us that nothing has to stay the same, including our health. We can transform it from poor to excellent by infusing our body with optimal nutrition!

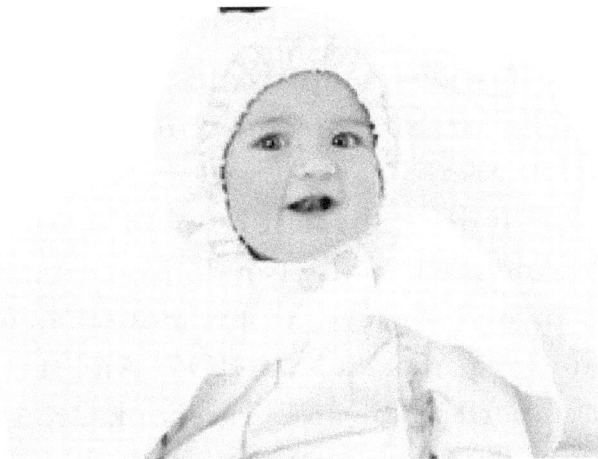

DRESSING UP IN COSTUME is something kids and adults alike get to do openly, creatively, and without commitment for any more than a night. We can try on a new mask or take the opportunity to outwardly ridicule or celebrate a public personality. We can be whomever, or whatever, we want to be - our imagination is the only limit!

How about encouraging your guests to dress up in a healthy food related costume? There is substantial evidence to show that children who participate in preparing their own meals are more likely to eat them, even when nutritious! Perhaps the same theory holds true for those who fabricate or wear a healthy food related costume! A chef? A banana? A pumpkin? What else?

TRICK-OR-TREATING The act of going door to door dressed in costume usually marks the beginning of the end of the Halloween activities. This popular tradition has the power to turn strangers into friends, isolation into community. Trick-or-Treating is unique in that it involves going out of your way to interact with people you've never met before. You buy candy or toys for children you don't know, and celebrate alongside neighbors for perhaps the first time. It reminds us that even though we're often separated from others, we do in fact enjoy giving, being creative, and celebrating together!

On the dark side of this tradition is the fact that while those costumed visitors make small threats of pranks (trick) if not given a small gift (treat), the real threat usually lies within the gifts themselves. Traditionally, most treats are candy - loaded with the evils of trans fats, genetically modified sugar, artificial colors, and artificial flavorings. Those toxic ingredients contribute to many of the health issues experienced by children today, including overweight and obesity.

BEWARE of Fake Foods

Food advertising has led us to eat things that look like food but are filled with artificial sweeteners and colors. Halloween, the second biggest commercial holiday in the US, serves as the perfect time for candy companies to sell their processed treats. Many candies use corn syrup, additives, food coloring, and hydrogenated fats. Together, these ingredients increase disease risk, especially for diabetes mellitus, obesity, heart disease, and various cancers.

We are human beings dependent upon food for life living on a planet. Let's gather ingredients and choose whovle foods wisely, for the health of people and our planet.

Corn Syrup and Excess Sugar

High-fructose corn syrup is a common sweetener, widely available as a result of surplus corn agriculture. With the advent of corn syrup, sugar consumption has increased to as much as 150 pounds per person per year. When you consume that much sugar, it becomes a toxin. Corn syrup contains other dangerous chemicals as well. Most notably, trace amounts of mercury from manufacturing end up in foods that use this sweetener. Though keep in mind, the Mayo Clinic warns that too much sugar of all kinds can contribute excess calories that lead to weight gain and metabolic diseases.

Additives and Food Coloring

Brian Wansink, head of Cornell University's Food and Brand Lab, concludes that visibility and convenience strongly influence how much we eat. Manufacturers rely on synthetic dyes as a inexpensive way to make food attractive, and with Halloween around the corner, various bright-colored candies are abundant and purposely enticing. Synthetic food dyes have been associated with childhood allergies, hyperactivity, learning impairments, and aggressiveness. You can check product ingredient lists for natural colorants, such as beet, carotenes, annatto, and turmeric. Avoid ingredients that list the color name - it's not natural.

Hydrogenated Fats

Trans fats, or hydrogenated fats, are naturally occurring fats (vegetable oils) that are blasted with hydrogen. This modification turns liquid oils into solids, extending the shelf life of many packaged foods, including several candies that may go into your trick-or-treat bucket. We are not intended to ingest these manufactured fats. The body does not know how to handle them, and they therefore increase the risk of disease. Since food manufacturers are not required to report trans fat amounts less than 0.5 g, you may be getting more trans fats than you believe. Each candy bar adds up! For this reason, it's best to avoid any treats that list hydrogenated or partially hydrogenated oil in their ingredient list.

Alternatives to the EVILS of Candy

While some parents will trade their children money or a toy for the bag of wicked treats, that bag of candy is usually passed along to the 'less fortunate,' who are already at higher risk for those diseases.

So... this Halloween, consider offering the goblins and ghouls that ring your doorbell nonfood items like Halloween straws, pencils, stickers, balloons, rub-on tattoos, keychains, erasers, and so on. It's easy to find big bags of them at low prices at local party supply and dollar stores. If you're intent on providing edible treats, why not use healthier snacks like pretzels, popcorn, low sugar granola bars, or sugar free gum.

BOBBING FOR APPLES This classic Halloween activity involves filling a tub or large basin with water and putting in enough apples to cover most of the surface. The hands of the participant are tied behind his or her back so that he or she has only their teeth by which to grab the apple, either by biting onto the stem or into the flesh.

Imperfectly Vegan™: Halloween Style

The more adventurous or competitive may push the apple to the bottom or side of the basin in order to stabilize it for easier grabbing.

For those who desire, some education can accompany this game with the explanation as simple or complex as the participating minds will allow.

Why do apples float when on water?
Because they are less dense than water.

Does an apple contain cholesterol?
No! Because it comes from a plant! Plants do NOT contain cholesterol.

Does an apple contain fiber?
Yes! Because it comes from a plant! Plants DO contain fiber.

SPIDER WEB TOSS This game is fun for both kids and adults and can serve as a nice ice-breaker. That is, as a way to introduce people to one another. All you need is a big ball of white yarn and some enthusiastic participants. To play, everyone stands in a circle that is wide enough to toss a ball of white yarn to one another. The first person with the yarn can say his or her name, for example, and then toss the ball to someone else in the circle. The person who catches it then states their name and tosses it to someone else. This continues until everyone has had a chance to say their name. Then, depending upon the number of people and how complex a web you wish to weave, the play can continue with a different question to be answered. The questions can be simple, silly, or serious to match your guests' age and interests. As you can imagine, by the end of the activity, a wonderful spider web has been woven! I like the symbolism of this activity because it demonstrates our interconnectedness. That, unlike a real spider, each one of us alone cannot create the web. It can only happen when we work together. And, each one of us doesn't have to do all that much to make a significant difference.

MUMMY MAKING CONTEST This is another fun game for kids and adults alike. I suppose, when it comes down to it, all games are fun so long as we can embrace our inner child! The object of this game is to see who can wrap up his or her mummy the fastest (and most complete). All you need are rolls of toilet paper (best to use an inexpensive sustainable brand) and masking tape (optional). Have your guests form teams of about 2-4 people each, depending upon the number of participants. One person will be mummified and the rest will work together to wrap the mummy. Each wrapper will get a roll of toilet paper. Tell them that if their toilet paper breaks, they can either roll over the broken piece, tie the broken ends back together, or use masking tape to connect the ends. Choose several other guests to be judges. Set a timer for ten minutes and watch them wrap! After the timer sounds, the judges can determine who made the best mummy. Take pictures or video them trying to walk. Of course, it will be a short video as toilet paper isn't nearly the strength of the fabric used to wrap the real deals.

Bean Bag Toss into plastic Jack-O-Lanterns   (Nutrition Info about BEANS: Types of beans/nutrient benefits)

Provide your goblins and ghouls with some **HALLOWEEN PUZZLES** to solve, either at the party or to take home. In fact, a printed puzzle would be an excellent substitute for candy for your neighborhood trick-or-treaters! See 19 Halloween Puzzles in the Appendix.

Halloween offers a great opportunity to gather friends to **WATCH A HORROR MOVIE**. And the vegan movement offers a unique reason to view frightening images while being educated about the horrors of animal cruelty and the unnecessarily devastating consequences of a poor diet. Below are some recommended films for this purpose. *NOTE: SOME OF THESE FILMS ARE NOT APPROPRIATE FOR YOUNG CHILDREN!*

King Corn
Fed Up
The Future of Food
Forks Over Knives

Cowspiracy
Earthlings
Dominion
Fridays at the Farm
Food Matters
Vegicated
Ingredients
Super Size Me
The World According to Monsanto
Tapped
Blue Gold: World Water Wars

For more Halloween games and activities, check out these links:

Halloween Games for Kids

https://www.thebalance.com/halloween-party-games-kids-1357658

Halloween Games for Adults

https://www.thebalance.com/adult-halloween-party-games-1357657

FOOD'S TRANSFORMATIVE POWER

Halloween serves as another example of this holiday's transformative capabilities through the FOOD that we enjoy at this time of year. Whether you're turning pumpkins into pumpkin pie, roasting nuts into a completely new toasty treat, or combining flour and spices to make traditional soul cakes, by cooking food you're already embracing and harnessing the art of transformation.

Food transforms us. As it does, may it lighten your path such that you shine brightly, much like the pumpkin turned jack-o-lantern.

One of the most exciting things about food, and therefore nutrition, is that it constantly exemplifies how the divine works all things together for good. Indeed, every nutrient needed for our most vibrant expression of health can be found within the foods that the Earth provides. It's not necessary to manufacture a single food. In fact, it is the official position of the American Academy of Nutrition and Dietetics that 'most healthy people can get all the nutrients they need from food in a well planned diet, and that the best nutrition based strategy for promoting optimal health and reducing the risk of chronic disease is to wisely choose a wide variety of nutrient-rich foods.'

However, most people realize that they do not consume enough healthy food, particularly fruits and vegetables. So what do we do? Well, at least 50 percent of Americans take a multivitamin every day, at a cost of over $20 billion per year. The use of dietary supplements in general, and nutrient supplements in particular, is prevalent and growing in the United States, but multivitamins have been shown to be practically useless, and can in fact be hazardous to your health. Turns out they may be more trick than treat!

First, foods contain substances that are not available from nutritional supplements. Supplements contain only those nutrients that scientists have discovered and have been able to extract and put into sellable capsules, tablets, gels, and powders. But there are thousands of important compounds that simply have not been discovered yet, or that scientists haven't figured out how to isolate and put in a pill. A well-known saying amongst nutritionists is "If science could create a pill that gave us all the vitamins and minerals we need, the only problem would be swallowing it!" It's important to remember that supplements are just that—products intended to supplement the nutritional value of your diet, not replace nor serve as its primary source.

Second, food provides the synergy that many nutrients require for efficient use by the body. The term "synergy" refers to the action of two or more substances or organisms coming together to achieve an effect that each is incapable of achieving alone. Food provides us nutrition that is more than the sum of its parts! While the RDA for vitamin C is sixty milligrams (enough to prevent scurvy and other deficiency diseases), much higher levels are often recommended for optimal health. However, since vitamin C is a water-soluble vitamin and the body can absorb only about two hundred milligrams at one time, intakes above this amount literally go down the drain through urine. That means, money down the drain, too!

Isolated Nutrients vs. Whole Foods

To underscore the difference between isolated nutrients and whole food, the small amount of vitamin C in an apple, about six milligrams, along with the total amount of antioxidants, is as effective at reducing oxidative stress as 1,300 milligrams of isolated vitamin C. That's the power of synergy! As another example, we absorb more of the plant-based non-heme iron when we consume it along with vitamin C. Additionally, carotenoids, the precursor to vitamin A, are better absorbed when consumed with fat, since many are fat soluble. I imagine there are countless other examples of food synergy that have yet to be discovered. By eating a wide variety of whole plant foods, we optimize our chances of benefiting from them all.

The Failure of High Dose Synthetic Vitamins

One of the most significant studies to awaken researchers and health care providers to the importance of food synergy is the Beta-Carotene and Retinol Efficacy Trial (CARET). Because observational studies suggest that people eating more fruits and vegetables rich in beta-carotene and retinol have lower rates of lung cancer, researchers wanted to test the effects of such natural compounds in isolated form, so they administered high dosages of vitamins to more than eighteen thousand people at high risk for cancer and death from smoking and asbestos exposure. Half of the subjects were given an "intervention" of vitamins, while the other half received a placebo (no vitamin intervention). During the study, researchers found that those given the vitamins had a 28 percent increase in lung cancer, a 17 percent increase in death, and an increased risk of cardiovascular disease, compared with the group that did not receive the vitamins. Because the trial presented no clear evidence of benefit and substantial evidence of possible harm, the researchers terminated it in 1996, twenty-one months earlier than planned, and took all subjects off the vitamin intervention.

CARET is just one of an increasing number of studies that have found isolated vitamins to be ineffective and dangerous. Fortunately, the media is getting the word out! This standpoint is supported by UC Berkeley's School of Public Health's Wellness Report 2016: Dietary Supplements, which states that many popular nutrition supplements are not as effective as had been thought, including our daily multivitamin pill. A large systematic review (a study that takes data from multiple studies) released in 2018 looked at 179 individual studies to find if taking supplemental vitamins and minerals had any effect on cardiovascular disease outcomes and all cause mortality (death). They concluded that these supplements provided no benefit, and instead recommended a "move toward more plant-based diets that are relatively rich in vitamins and minerals." Further, the US government neither regulates supplements nor tests supplements for safety or effectiveness. Supplement manufacturers are not required to list exact nutrients and quantities of nutrients on their labels, nor are they required to prove a product's safety and efficacy before they release it into the marketplace. Scary! Also, the word "natural" on a label does not mean that the product is safe, and false claims like "boosts stamina," "arouses sexual desire" and "enhances muscle tone" can be listed on the label without any supporting evidence.

The FDA - No Protection Against Chemical "Vitamins"

Finally, the FDA does not require supplements to carry warning labels regarding any potential side effects, which include dizziness, nausea, blurred vision, muscle cramps, headache, constipation, difficulty breathing, insomnia, decreased libido, and tremors. What's behind these findings? Essentially, the constituents of food are most biologically active when they are provided in whole-food form and can be ineffective and toxic when isolated. Just as a scary movie is only effective when it combines sound and sight, the body is only effectively nourished by food that provides various nutrients. Have you ever watched the movie Jaws on mute? Without the ominous "da-da...da-da," the film becomes a bunch of silly scenes with an obviously animatronic shark and fake blood. It's the whole experience of terror building music and frightful imagery that creates fear in the viewer - if each are isolated, the film becomes ridiculous and cheesy. Similarly, isolating a single nutrient from food does not allow it to serve the body as intended.

Food is the Best Medicine, NOT Pills That Try (and Fail)

Evolutionarily, humans tell each other about foods that make them sick, not individual nutrients. Dietary supplements containing isolated vitamins or minerals do not have the same beneficial effects as food itself. Consider that the average multivitamin supplement contains thirty-one nutrients. Consuming a multivitamin is like having thirty pieces of a ten-thousand-piece puzzle -- can you put the puzzle together? No. And having high doses of a single nutrient, like vitamin C, is like having one thousand identical puzzle pieces. Again, can you assemble the puzzle? No. What we need to solve the puzzle is thousands of unique pieces, each in small amounts, that fit together. In human life, what the body needs is what a variety of plants, especially fruit and vegetables, provide - tens of thousands of unique compounds that work together synergistically.

There are special cases, however, in which taking an isolated nutrient is recommended, such as a B12 supplement for vegans. This need has more to do with a changing agricultural landscape with fewer B12 producing bacteria in the soil than an inherent deficiency in the diet.

Generally, our bodies assimilate nutrients most effectively when we eat them in their natural state - whole foods.

A Special Message About Your Personal Transformation

Do you want to change your shape?

Do you want to detoxify your body?

Do you want to lose unhealthy and unwanted fat?

Do you want brighter clearer skin?

Do you want more energy?

Are you ready to clean your haunted house?

Join our ImperfectlyVegan™ Facebook Group

Get the support you need to transform your health and improve your well-being.

The purpose of this group is to share knowledge and provide support to help you and your family shift to better health, in part, by adopting a more vegan lifestyle. Being "ImperfectlyVegan™" is an approach to eating that mutually benefits our individual, communal, and environmental well-being. In this group we'll share knowledge, camaraderie, recipes, and all kinds of practical knowledge.

Being ImperfectlyVegan™ means following a plant-based diet as much as possible without getting hung up or giving up if you eat a small amount of animal food. It is about making a commitment to all of life. The degree to which someone is ImperfectlyVegan™ depends on his or her personal level of commitment, experience, and circumstances, all of which may change at different points in time. While the health advantages of a vegetarian diet compared with those of a non-vegetarian diet are well documented and highly significant, when it comes to giving up eggs and small amounts of dairy, those differences are not as significant. However, being ImperfectlyVegan™ is about following a plant-based diet for more than health reasons. It is a spiritual approach to life that honors life, including those of animals.

Being ImperfectlyVegan™ is a lifestyle, not a destination. Welcome and join the conversation.

RECIPES FOR A
TASTY TRANSFORMATION

1. Pumpkin Harvest Soup

2. Roasted Tomato Spread

3. Protein Powered PUMPKIN Pie Pancakes

4. SCREAMY Chocolate Mousse

5. Chocolate Chip BOO-nana Bread

6. Spicy Toasted Pecans – aka BAT BRAINS

7. BOO-nana Muffins

8. PUMPKIN Muffins

9. Dark as Night Brownies

10. EYEBALL Punch

11. CAULDRON Caramel Apples

12. BAT Fruit Salad

Imperfectly Vegan™: Halloween Style

Pumpkin Harvest Soup

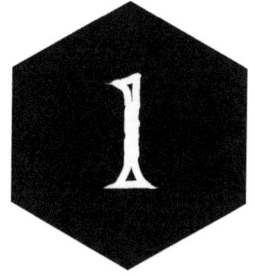

Nothing says Fall like soup. This delicious soup lets you enjoy some of the best produce the season has to offer - it's like having the harvest in a bowl!

Makes 12 servings (you may want to freeze half for another time).

Ingredients:

1 small yellow onion, peeled and sliced

3" piece ginger (or more as desired), peeled and sliced into 1/4" pieces

6-8 cloves garlic, peeled

3 Fuji or other sweet apples, peeled and cut in quarters

2 sweet pears, peeled and cut in half or quarters

3 medium sweet potatoes, peeled and cut into 1/2" pieces

2 large carrots, peeled and cut into 3" pieces

1/2 medium pumpkin/butternut squash OR 1 can organic pumpkin

2 tbsp organic coconut oil

2 tsp margarine

2 tsp salt

4 oz water OR white wine

6 cups water

Directions:

1. Peel pumpkin, sweet potatoes, carrots, apples, pears, onion and ginger and roughly chop into 3" pieces.
2. Heat coconut oil and margarine in large sauté pan over medium heat.
3. Add cut items and garlic to pan.
4. Stir to coat pieces with coconut oil and margarine.
5. Sprinkle with salt.
6. Turn heat to medium-high and cover with a lid. Allow everything to brown, stirring occasionally. Scrape the bottom of the pan from time to time.
7. Once browned, add 4 oz water or white wine to pan and continue to cook with lid on. Cook until tender (easily pierced with a fork), about 25 minutes.
8. Remove from heat and put into blender or food processor about ⅓ of sautéed ingredients at a time. If using canned pumpkin, add it now. Add 2 cups water (distilled or filtered) to each batch to help liquify. You can adjust the amount of water added to make the soup as thick or thin as you desire. Just keep in mind that diluting it too much may change flavor.
9. Add salt to taste.
10. ENJOY!

Recipe by Lisa Tremont Ota

2 ROASTED TOMATO SPREAD

This one's a new family tradition and staple! I like to quadruple the recipe so that I can freeze portions for future use.

Ingredients:

2 28-oz cans organic peeled whole plum tomatoes (without added basil and salt)
1/2 cup organic extra-virgin olive oil (EVOO)
1/2 cup red onion, finely chopped

6 cloves garlic, coarsely chopped
1 1/2 tsp fine sea salt
2 tsp dried basil
1 tsp fresh rosemary, crumbled
1/2 tsp freshly ground pepper

Directions:

1. Preheat oven to 350 degrees. Line a baking sheet with a silicone liner.
2. Dump the canned tomatoes into a strainer or colander over a large ceramic or glass bowl. Pour the drained juice into containers that can be kept in the freezer so that you can use it for tomato sauce or soup or juice some other time.
3. Quarter the drained tomatoes and place in a large glass bowl (perhaps the one from which you just reserved the tomato juice).
4. Stir into the tomatoes the olive oil, basil, rosemary, onion, garlic, salt and pepper, being careful not to tear the tomatoes.
5. Pour the mixture onto the lined pan and bake for 1 - 1½ hours, stirring every 20 minutes (maybe more often towards the end) and checking to be sure that the tomatoes and garlic don't brown/burn.
6. Transfer the roasted tomatoes to a glass bowl and let mellow at room temperature for about 6 hours.
7. Refrigerate for up to 4 days, or freeze for up to 3 months.

Works great as:

a topping on crostini
a substitute in many recipes that call for tomatoes or tomato paste or sundried tomatoes
a soup flavor enhancement
over pasta (a little goes a long way)
as a topping on toast as an open-faced sandwich

Recipe by Lisa Tremont Ota

PROTEIN POWERED PUMPKIN PIE PANCAKES

3

This is the perfect power breakfast, great for enjoying the flavors of fall. Between the protein powder, cashews, and oats, these pancakes are hardy and filling. At the same time, they're well rounded with a slight sweetness and hint of spice. Plus they're gluten free, soy free, and vegan!

Makes 6 pancakes.

Ingredients:

1/2 cup oats
1/2 cup cashewsImage result for pumpkin clipart black and white
1 tsp baking powder
1/2 cup vanilla protein powder
1 tsp cinnamon
1/8 tsp cloves

1/8 tsp nutmeg
3/4 cup canned pumpkin
2 tbsp coconut sugar
1/2 cup plant milk
Pinch of sea salt
Coconut oil for heating pan
Optional: pure maple syrup for topping

Directions:

1. Blend cashews and oats until a fine flour consistency is achieved. Add baking powder and protein powder and blend until evenly mixed. Transfer mixture to a large bowl, or continue adding ingredients to blender/ food processor.
2. Add remainder of ingredients and mix or blend until all ingredients are distributed in batter.
3. Heat a frying pan on low-medium heat and add a tsp of oil to coat the pan.
4. Add 1/4 cup batter to center of pan and spread with a rubber spatula into desired shape. Heat for approximately 3 minutes, or until batter appears dry.
5. Flip and cook another 3 minutes, or until both sides are golden brown.
6. Top with pure maple syrup, if desired, for the full fall-flavor experience.

FUN FACT: Did you know that pumpkins have more potassium than bananas? This makes them great for refueling post workout, as potassium is an important electrolyte that keeps your muscles performing at their best. They're also a high source of vitamin A, which aids in vision, especially at night.

Recipe by Reilly Gardine

4 SCREAMY CHOCOLATE MOUSSE

Avocados aren't just for salads and guacamolé! While travelling in Byron Bay, Australia, in the spring of 2017, I made an intention to increase my repertoire of vegan desserts. As the universe would have it, I was introduced to Jeani-Rose Atchison at the Farmer's Market. Recognizing that we shared a passion for plant-based eating for the purposes of nurturing our individual, communal, and environmental well-being, we signed and exchanged copies of our books. Her book included this vegan dessert which, with small modifications, has become a staple in my household. My son actually asks me to make this... on a regular basis! As such, I order a box of 5.4 ounce cans of coconut cream on Amazon so that I can have what I need on hand. Super easy and fast to make! No baking required!

Makes 6-8 3/4 cup servings.

Ingredients:
6 medium avocados
½ cup cacao powder
⅓ cup coconut cream or 1 5.4 fluid oz can

1/2 cup agave
1 tbsp organic vanilla
Pinch sea salt

Directions:
1. Quarter avocados, removing seed and peel. Place avocado 'meat' into food processor and run until creamy.
2. Add all remaining ingredients, continuing to run until well mixed.
3. Add more sweetener (agave), vanilla, or cacao as desired.
4. Portion equally into small cups.
5. Chill in refrigerator (though it may also be enjoyed immediately if you just can't wait).

Original recipe from Food for Thought Thought for Food by Jeani-Rose Atchison

CHOCOLATE CHIP BOO-NANA BREAD

5

Growing up, my mom made banana bread so much it almost became a staple in my life. My family eats bunches of bananas like nothing, but of course there will be a couple of overripe, spotty bananas that no one wants to eat anymore. My mother makes a non-vegan banana bread recipe, but this vegan recipe is equally yummy!

Makes 10 servings.

Ingredients:

4 medium overripe bananas
1/2 cup sunflower oil
1/2 cup coconut sugar
1 tsp vanilla extract
1 tsp cinnamon

1 1/2 cups whole wheat flour
1 1/2 tsp baking powder
1/2 tsp baking soda
1/2 cup vegan chocolate chips
Non-stick cooking spray

Directions:

1. Preheat oven to 350 degrees. Grease loaf pan.
2. Add peeled bananas, oil, sugar, vanilla, and cinnamon to large bowl and mix evenly.
3. Mix flour, baking powder, and baking soda into another large bowl.
4. Fold the wet mixture into the dry mixture (do not over-mix). Fold in the chocolate chips.
5. Pour the batter into the pan evenly. Bake at 350 degrees for 30-45 minutes (until toothpick comes out clean). 6. Let cool for 15 minutes.
7. Slice & serve!

COOKS NOTE: This recipe is absolutely delicious as-is, but feel free to substitute and it will be just as good:
• use any kind of oil (coconut, grapeseed, olive, etc.)
• use any kind of sugar (brown, white, etc.)
• use any kind of flour (almond, oat, gluten free all purpose, etc)
• use any kind of mix-ins (nuts, sunflower seeds, raisins, etc)
• if skipping mix-ins, coat the top with a mixture of cinnamon and sugar

Carefully watch the time on this. Undercooked is better than overcooked. Set the timer for 30 minutes and then check on it every 5 minutes until done. If the crust is browning and the middle is still gooey, cover in aluminum foil until cooked more thoroughly.

Recipe adapted by Leandra Padayachee

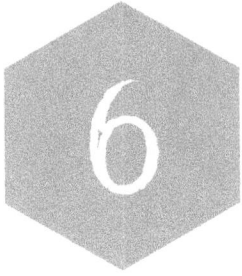

6 SPICY TOASTED PECANS — AKA BAT BRAINS

(A nourishing two-day process)

While Native Americans collected and stored pecans for long periods during the cold winter months when food was scarce, we can pretty much find halves and pieces year round. Pecans were also used to trade for other goods. In a related fashion, I like to express my gratitude to my hairdresser, gardener, and children's teachers by giving them a small bag of Spicy Toasted Pecans, a recipe passed along to me by my dear friend, Sarah. They are delicious on salads, soups, sweet potatoes, and just by themselves!

Ingredients:

1 lb pecans
3 tbsp melted margarine (Smart Balance or other type)
1/3 cup sugar (do not use coconut sugar)
1 tbsp Karo syrup
1 ts pure vanilla extract

1/2 tsp salt
1/4 tsp pepper
1/2 tsp cinnamon
1/2 tsp allspice
1/4 tsp ground nutmeg
1/2 tsp coriander

Directions Day 1:

Bring water to a boil. Add 1 lb pecans and let boil for 1 minute. Drain and put in a bowl.
Stir in the melted margarine, sugar, Karo syrup, vanilla extract
Put on a non-stick cookie sheet and leave on counter overnight.

Directions Day 2:

Preheat oven to 300 degrees.
Bake pecans for 40 minutes, stirring every 10 minutes. Be sure to set your timer each time!
When done, put into a bowl and toss with the salt, pepper, cinnamon, allspice, ground nutmeg, and coriander.

Put back onto baking sheet to cool. Share and enjoy!

Original recipe by Sarah Pepper Block

Adapted by Lisa Tremont Ota

BOO-NANA MUFFINS

Makes 12 muffins.

Ingredients:

3 - 4 ripe bananas, smashedImage result for halloween clipart black and white
1/3 cup melted organic margarine
3/4 cup organic sugar
1 tbs flax seed with 2 Tbsp. warm water
1 ts vanilla

1 ts baking soda
Pinch of salt
3/4 cup finely ground raw walnuts (food processor works well)
3/3 cup whole wheat flour

Directions:

1. Preheat the oven to 350d degrees. With a wooden spoon, mix margarine into the mashed bananas in a large mixing bowl.
2. Mix the flaxseed with warm water, then mix into bananas along with the sugar and vanilla.
3. Sprinkle the baking soda and salt over the mixture and mix in.
4. Add the flour, mix until it is just incorporated. Fold in the finely ground walnuts.
5. Pour mixture into nonstick muffin tin. Bake for 25-30 minutes. Insert toothpick into the center of a muffin to test for doneness. If it comes out clean, it's done. Cool on wire rack.

COOK'S TIP: Seeds and nuts are whole foods, which makes shopping for them easy. When shopping, remember the following:
• Buy these items from bins whenever possible, since this will prevent the unnecessary purchase of plastics and containers that add to landfills. You will also be more likely to purchase just the amount you need and will thereby avoid having to throw away any excess that has gone bad over time. This method almost always costs less, too!
• Choose unsalted varieties to avoid excess sodium.

Recipe by Lisa Tremont Ota

8 PUMPKIN MUFFINS

With just 170 calories per standard muffin, less than five grams of fat, and no cholesterol, these little pumpkins pack in nutrition with healthy doses of essential polyunsaturated fatty acids, iron, calcium, vitamin C, beta-carotene, and fiber! Bake them in mini bundt pans to make pumpkin shaped muffins (pictured here), twelve-cup muffin tins for the ideal single serving size, or in loaf pans for more surface area to toast when sliced. I created the recipe for these pumpkin muffins over twenty years ago by applying some of the principles I had learned while taking a food science course at CAL. Now I bake them for my boys. I guess that gives new meaning to how good nutrition before pregnancy can impact our children.

Makes 12 muffins.

Ingredients:

3/4 cup oat bran
3/4 cup whole wheat flour
1/2 cup granulated sugar
1 1/2 tsp cinnamon
1 tsp baking powder
1 tsp baking soda
1/2 tsp salt

1 cup raisins
1 cup canned or cooked pumpkin
2 tbsp agar mixed with 2 tbsp water
1/4 cup vegetable oil
2/3 cup plain non-dairy yogurt

Directions:

1. Mix together all the dry ingredients listed above, including the raisins.
2. In a separate bowl, mix together the remaining wet ingredients.
3. Then add the wet mixture to the dry mixture. Stir just until combined.
4. Spoon batter into a paper lined or nonstick muffin tin. (Use a tin with mini bundt cakes to make pumpkin shaped muffins!) Bake at 400 degrees for 25 minutes.

COOK'S TIP: I like to double or triple this recipe so that I have a dozen or two to freeze.

Recipe by Lisa Tremont Ota

DARK AS NIGHT BROWNIES

Both cakey AND fudgy, these ultra-dark chocolate brownies are a delicious treat - though you've been forewarned, they're super dark and rich! The coffee in this recipe enhances the brownie's chocolatey flavor, a great tip to incorporate in your other chocolate treats. Add cinnamon if you like a little warmth in your dessert, it gives these brownies an unexpected spice.

Ingredients:

1/2 cup almond milk

1/4 cup brewed coffee (I used cold brew)

1/2 cup maple syrup

1 tbsp vanilla extract

2 tbsp ground flaxseed

1/4 cup sunflower oil

1/2 cup vegan yogurt

1 cup gluten free flour

1 cup cacao or cocoa powder

3/4 tsp baking powder

1/3 cup coconut sugar

1/2 tsp sea salt

1/2 cup dark (>70%) mini chocolate chips

Optional: 2 tsp ground cinnamon for a warming twist

Directions:

1. Preheat oven to 330°F.
2. Line a baking pan with parchment paper.
3. Whisk together all wet ingredients + flaxseed, set aside for ~5 minutes.
4. In a separate bowl combine all other ingredients, except chocolate chips.
5. Combine both wet and dry ingredients, mixing until combined. Fold in the mini chips.
6. Bake for ~20 minutes.
7. Cool and eat!

Recipe by Reilly Gardine

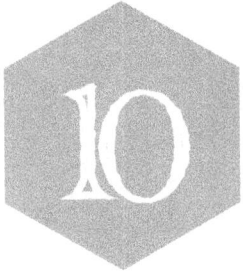

10 EYEBALL PUNCH

What could be spookier than a bunch of eyeballs floating around in your punch?! Gross out your party guests with this delicious and refreshing drink, which is as fun to make as it is to sip! If you're having an adult party, feel free to spike it with an alcohol of your choice, though remember it's recommended that most men stick to two drinks a day, and most women stick to just one.

Ingredients:

Canned lychee fruit (usually found in the Asian section of the store)

Fresh blueberries (preferably organic)

3 cups 100% juice (try blueberry, pomegranate, or other juices with a red tint to them)

3 cups sparkling water (any flavor)

1/3 cup liquid from the lychee fruit can

Juice of three limes

Ice

Optional: 1 cup vodka, gin, or any clear liquor of your choice

Directions:

1. Stick one to two blueberries in the cavity of each lychee. These are your "eyeballs." Make as many as you want to fill your punch bowl or jar. These can be super fun for kids to make.

2. Stir together juice, lychee liquid, and lime juice, plus liquor if you're using it. Add sparkling water and lightly stir.

3. Pour this mixture into a punch bowl full of ice, or store in a large jar to pour into individual glasses filled with ice.

4. Add in your "eyeballs," and enjoy your creepy drink!

Recipe by Reilly Gardine

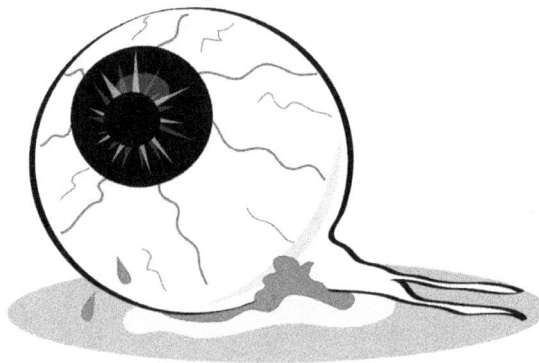

Imperfectly Vegan™: Halloween Style

CAULDRON CARAMEL APPLES

You can still enjoy most childhood treats as a vegan, just a few substitutions required! These candied apples are reminiscent of the sweet caramel apples found during the fall season, minus the butter and cream. Featuring more of a brittle candy coating than chewy caramel, this apple based dessert is sure to satisfy your sweet tooth. Feel free to jazz up these treats even more by rolling your candied apples in any topping of your choice before the caramel has cooled - think shredded coconut, cacao nibs, crushed peanuts - the options are endless!

Makes 4 apples.

Ingredients:
1 cup sugar
1/4 cup coconut oil
3 tbsp soy milk
1/8 tsp cream of tartar
1/8 tsp salt
1/4 tsp vanilla extract
4 apples, with imbedded popsicle stick or skewer

Directions:
1. Whisk together all ingredients except apples in a small saucepan on medium heat until oil is melted and all sugar is dissolved. Continue heating until boiling and then turn to low.
2. Continue to occasionally stir caramel sauce on low heat until mixture is a warm brown color. Allow to cool for ~5 minutes, or until mixture is cool enough to touch. It should be thick.
3. Return sauce to heat, until bubbling, and continue heating while stirring for about a minute. Remove from heat and begin to coat apples in caramel sauce once it has thickened enough to stick to the apples. You'll have to coat the apples quickly, as the sauce thickens pretty rapidly.
4. Place finished candied apples on a baking sheet lined with parchment paper and allow to fully cool before eating. You can speed up the cooling process by placing apples in the fridge.

Original recipe by Monica of The Hidden Veggies
Adapted by Reilly Gardine

12 BAT FRUIT SALAD

This one needs little explanation. Gather your favorite fruits and call them by their Halloween names. For example, bananas = BOOnanas; cantaloupe = CADAVERloupe; blueberries = BOOberries. Enjoy!

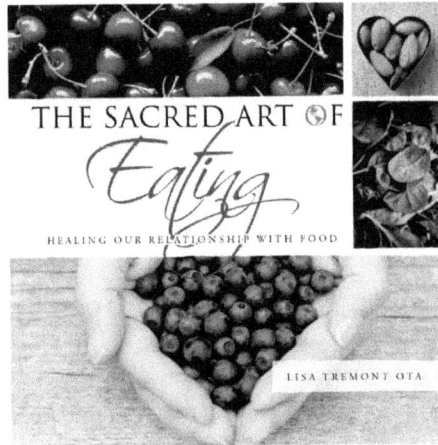

Want more great ideas about a vegan lifestyle and even how to hold a vegan dinner party?
Check out The Sacred Art of Eating

Want to join a like-minded people going vegan and share support and ideas?
Join the Imperfectly Vegan Facebook group

Follow us on Twitter for great tips, recipes and more.

HALLOWEEN FOOD JOKES

1. Where do ghosts buy their food?
The ghostery store.

2. What do skeletons say before dining?
Bone Appetit!

3. What is a ghost's favorite breakfast?
Scream of wheat.

4. What is a vampire's favorite candy?
A sucker.

5. Why wasn't there any food left after the
Because Everyone was A Goblin.

6. What is a ghost's favorite dessert?
Boo-berry pie and I scream.

7. What is a ghost's favorite fruit?
Booberries.

8. What's the ratio of a pumpkin's circum
Pumpkin Pi.

9. What is a ghost's favorite dessert?
Boo-berry pie and I scream.

10. What is a vampire's favorite fruit?
A neck-tarine.

11. What do you call a witch that lives by the sea?
A sandwitch.

12. What to cannibals eat for dessert?
Chocolate covered aunts.

Word Search

The following words can be found in the diagram below reading forward, backward, up, down and diagonally. Find the words and circle them.

cat	knife
witch	moonlight
dead	spell
gourd	haunted
horror	tradition
goblin	skeleton

```
J T R M O O N L I G H T C S J A
C M R W Y G O B L I N M R R M I
A L U A G S U H W S P E L L Q X
T D E A D R R Z Z C V H C F Z E
X I E K F I C X W U K F F E L Y
Y S U P P M T G P L I K T K Q S
P O A U Y G W I V C R F H W K T
V I L Q X B C E O Q O N B H Y S
A N G B H F H E N N A K V G S S
R L R N Z W D X Y O F B O U O Q
W B O N I B A P C I T U J M V T
I I R C M B T K N I F E X O S U
T R R Q S X S H R H Y T L U H V
C G O U R D U W X D Q H Q E L B
H Z H N N A G L O Z F G Q Y K E
I F W H A U N T E D P D P J L S
```

Cryptogram

Each of these Cryptograms is a message in substitution code. THE SILLY DOG might become UJD WQPPZ BVN if U is substituted for T, J for H, D for E, etc. One way to break the code is to look for repeated letters. E, T, A, O, N, R and I are the most often used letters. A single letter is usually A or I; OF, IS and IT are common 2-letter words; try THE or AND for a 3-letter group. The code is different for each Cryptogram.

1. Ahvatqcr uzn uc nplniincw ryhzln ys
   enwu-luzywncn, wxn aiucw aznlhzryz
   ys gqwuvqc U.

2. Vmnb os usi xnee vhbxmdf bmnb ehtd
   bscdbmdz? Gzssk-knbdf!

3. Akis yf cfe riuu i ahsrk skis uhlbg
   pc skb gbi? I gixyahsrk.

Alphabet Soup

Insert a different letter of the alphabet into each of the 26 empty boxes to form words reading across. The letter you insert may be at the beginning, the end or the middle of the word. Each letter of the alphabet will be used only once. Cross off each letter in the list as you use it. All the letters in each row are not necessarily used in forming the word.

Example: In the first row, we have inserted the letter Z to form the word HAZELNUT

A B C D E F G H I J K L M N O P Q R S T U V W X Y Z̶

Y	G	O	Q	H	A	**Z**	E	L	N	U	T	L
R	E	W	P	O	I		O	N	O	G	H	J
U	R	R	W	O	L		Q	W	J	N	J	B
H	Q	M	V	Y	T		R	I	L	L	U	P
H	T	P	T	R	A		I	T	I	O	N	O
Q	Y	D	E	G	T		O	N	S	T	E	R
B	N	X	J	Z	S		U	L	L	O	L	L
O	I	S	O	U	L		N	G	Q	I	J	D
T	O	M	B	S	T		N	E	C	K	U	J
H	B	C	A	N	D		C	O	R	N	N	J
W	J	N	S	L	S		I	D	E	R	A	P
B	R	S	R	D	O		A	N	T	E	R	N
W	B	U	S	C	A		Y	M	Z	Y	Q	G
H	M	Q	C	L	M		O	B	L	I	N	F
U	A	E	G	M	S		U	A	B	F	X	F
Q	E	R	V	C	M		M	M	Y	X	S	E
H	E	M	M	D	E		D	L	K	H	L	F
V	E	S	W	W	E		M	R	U	C	P	V
Z	V	D	B	L	A		K	V	D	G	O	H
N	P	D	I	V	I		A	T	I	O	N	W
Q	E	T	D	C	A		W	E	E	M	Y	F
A	H	A	U	N	T		D	U	A	N	G	L
H	W	G	O	G	W		I	T	C	H	S	Z
R	F	E	C	A	R		E	P	W	K	H	A
P	U	X	B	A	N		O	H	M	O	D	V
A	O	D	E	B	E		I	L	E	C	K	R

Dittos

Form 5 different 5-letter words by using all the given letters and adding the letter in the Free Letter Box as often as necessary. Cross off each letter in the Letter Bank as you use it.

Free Letter	Letter Bank
d	a b b c e g g h i i k l l l n o o o r t u v

1. ___ ___ ___ ___ ___

2. ___ ___ ___ ___ ___

3. ___ ___ ___ ___ ___

4. ___ ___ ___ ___ ___

5. ___ ___ ___ ___ ___

Piece By Piece

The spaces between the words in the following message have been eliminated and divided into pieces. Rearrange the pieces to reconstruct the messages. The dashes indicate the number of letters in each word.

```
LAZ  LAS  YBO  CAL  TDO  KEL  NES
NTG  ETA  WHA  YOU  OWO  JOB  NWH
ETO
```

— — — —   — —   — — —

— — — —   —   — — — — — — —

— — —   — — — '—

— — —   —   — — — ?

— — — —   — — — — — !

Word Scramble

Below is a list of scrambled words. Unscramble all the letters to reveal the words.

1. CWHIT = _____

2. VRCEA = _____

3. MYUMM = _____

4. TCA = _____

5. LIAYDOH = _____

6. ENMOD = _____

7. SEMCRA = _____

8. UMMYM = _____

Crypto Words

Each of these Crypto Words are writen in substitution code. SILLY might become WQPPZ if S is substituted for W, I for Q, L for P, etc. When you have identified a word, use the known letters to decode the other words in the list.

HINT: m=a

1. APLOH = BONES

2. FMWJ = DARK

3. FOYPL = DEMON

4. QPRCPL = POTION

5. GOMFHRPLO = HEADSTONE

6. GMELROF = HAUNTED

7. MLBOU = ANGEL

8. BWMNOXMWF = GRAVEYARD

Key Words

To solve this puzzle, fill in the blanks below with the correct missing letter and then transfer the letter to the corresponding numbered square in the diagram below. Be careful! The puzzle is not as simple as it may first appear!

1.	2.	3.	4.	5.	6.	7.	8.

1. g h o _ t

2. m a _ e u p

3. k n i f _

4. c h i _ l

5. o r a n g _

6. n i g h _

7. b r _ o m

8. t u r _ i p

Two In

Place two letters on the dashes to complete a word on the left and to begin another word on the right. For example, SE in between PLEA and VEN would complete PLEASE and begin SEVEN.

1. w i t _ _ i l l

2. e r _ _ b l i n

3. h o r r _ _ a n g e

4. t a _ _ b w e b

5. g h o _ _ r e e t

Imperfectly Vegan™: Halloween Style

Flip Phone Mania

The below messages are in a number code based on how text messages are formed on a 'flip phone'. Each number represents one of the letters shown on the picture of the phone to the left. You must decide which one. A number is not necessarily the same letter each time.

1. 9428 47 2 32867483 33784628466 7768
    66 425569336? 5253 33743

2. 469 36 968 349 2 5225-6-5268376?
    9484 2 7867546 72824!

Interweave

Rearrange and distribute the four letters accompanying each row so that you form a larger common word.

1. a i d s : __ l l __ a __ n t s __ a y

2. b e l l : d o o r __ __ __ __

3. a n t e : h __ z __ l __ u __

4. a c r e : j __ __ k o l a n t __ __ n

5. e g o s : __ h __ __ t s t o r i __ s

Alphabet Soup

Insert a different letter of the alphabet into each of the 26 empty boxes to form words reading across. The letter you insert may be at the beginning, the end or the middle of the word. Each letter of the alphabet will be used only once. Cross off each letter in the list as you use it. All the letters in each row are not necessarily used in forming the word.

Example: In the first row, we have inserted the letter Z to form the word HAZELNUT

A B C D E F G H I J K L M N O P Q R S T U V W X Y Z̶

O	W	D	J	H	A	**Z**	E	L	N	U	T	L
J	Q	O	H	O	W		P	O	L	R	A	I
R	N	J	O	X	K		T	R	E	E	T	V
P	W	O	A	N	P		O	T	I	O	N	J
O	N	K	Z	B	O		X	W	J	A	G	Z
U	T	V	Z	C	A		V	E	Y	H	O	M
W	E	U	S	J	I		R	E	E	P	Y	P
Y	C	O	I	C	A		U	N	L	D	P	I
W	Z	R	L	O	C		O	B	E	R	A	E
X	G	R	A	V	E		A	R	D	U	Z	U
P	K	J	W	O	L		O	G	W	E	J	C
H	S	N	S	P	I		E	R	W	N	Z	J
P	W	J	D	L	E		U	A	L	B	R	Z
S	O	U	L	I	N		B	O	X	U	X	G
N	P	C	T	O	M		S	T	O	N	E	F
T	C	W	P	H	A		T	O	M	F	F	L
U	U	B	B	S	P		L	L	Z	L	Q	L
G	K	D	B	R	E		S	C	R	B	Q	O
I	Y	L	C	A	S		E	T	J	M	J	D
A	J	C	O	S	T		M	E	T	X	T	X
I	U	O	H	D	E		I	L	P	H	D	P
K	F	Y	X	B	C		I	L	L	M	W	K
L	L	L	K	C	E		I	T	S	W	L	G
G	R	V	A	M	P		R	E	M	H	R	Y
O	L	E	T	S	H		D	O	W	Y	Y	W
C	H	B	R	O	O		A	O	O	R	N	N

Bubble Words

Enter a single letter in each blank square in the diagrams below to form interlocking answers, each of which spell out distinct common words that differ only by the given pairs. See the example below to get a better idea. With the given arrangement of letters and blanks HOLE and HOST can be formed. More than one pair of words may appear to be possible, however the interlocking word will help eliminate the possibilites.

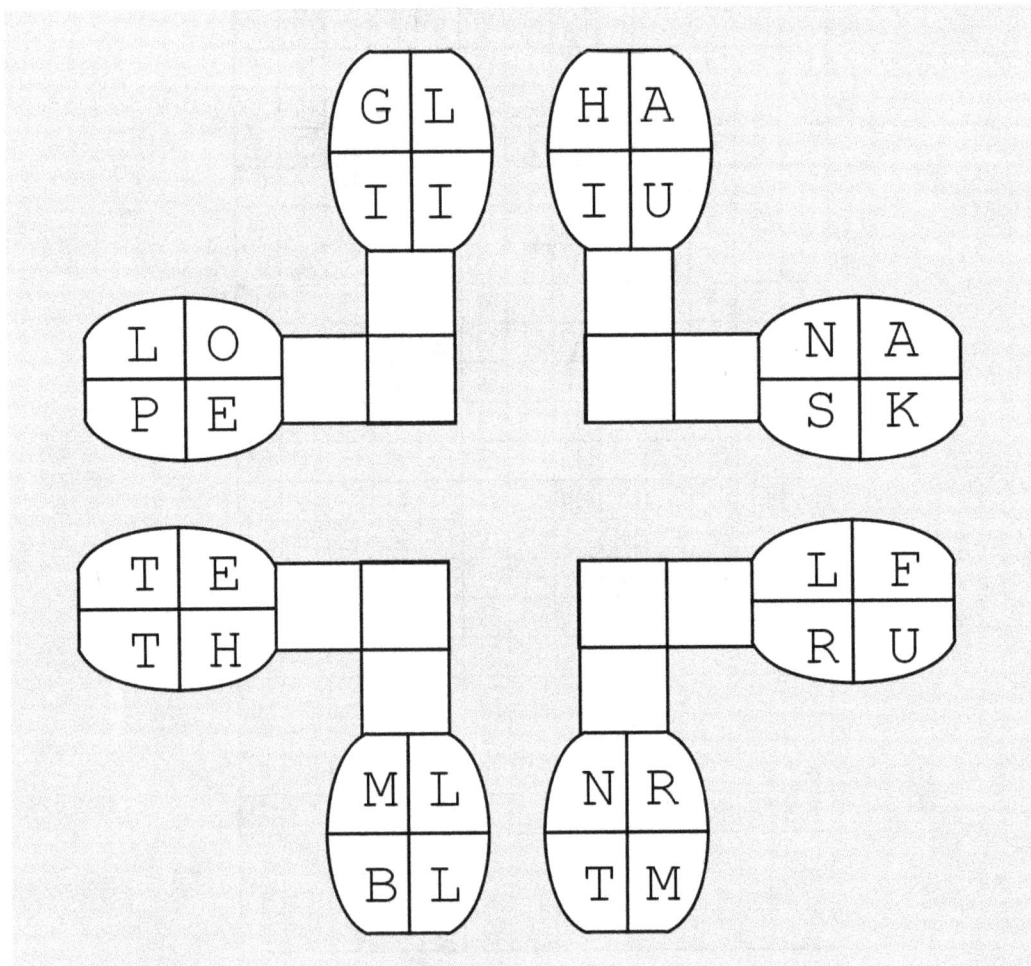

Piece By Piece

The spaces between the words in the following message have been eliminated and divided into pieces. Rearrange the pieces to reconstruct the messages. The dashes indicate the number of letters in each word.

```
ELE  WHA  PLA  ASK  VOR  TRU  MEN
TTO  OMB  INS  TIS  TON  SFA  ONE
YTR  ITE
```

— — — — — — —

— — — — — — — — ' —

— — — — — — — —

— — — — — — — — — —

— — — — — — ? — — — — — — — — !

Scramble

Below is a list of scrambled words. Unscramble all the letters to reveal the words.

1. NIGTH = _____

2. RSMTOEN = _____

3. NHEWOLEAL = _____

4. CARCDNNYO = _____

5. PLLSE = _____

6. GORDU = _____

7. ADUTHNE = _____

8. RBWE = _____

Crypto Words

Each of these Crypto Words are writen in substitution code. SILLY might become WQPPZ if S is substituted for W, I for Q, L for P, etc. When you have identified a word, use the known letters to decode the other words in the list.

HINT: r=a

1. QGRMLNY = _____

2. WRFI = _____

3. YDYYE = _____

4. HNFQKJ = _____

5. QDYQIVMURFY = _____

6. SJZ = _____

7. GNTVWRE = _____

8. YRKI = _____

Key Words

To solve this puzzle, fill in the blanks below with the correct missing letter and then transfer the letter to the corresponding numbered square in the diagram below. Be careful! The puzzle is not as simple as it may first appear!

1.	2.	3.	4.	5.	6.	7.	8.	9.

1. _ h r i l l

2. c i d e _

3. s c r e _ m

4. _ e v i l

5. s p _ d e r

6. n i g h _

7. p o _ s o n

8. t e r r _ r

9. d e m o _

Two In

Place two letters on the dashes to complete a word on the left and to begin another word on the right. For example, SE in between PLEA and VEN would complete PLEASE and begin SEVEN.

1. b e _ _ g e l

2. a c _ _ a d s t o n e

3. a m _ _ o n l i g h t

4. c h _ _ p l e

5. b a _ _ a d o w

Flip Phone Mania

The below messages are in a number code based on how text messages are formed on a 'flip phone'. Each number represents one of the letters shown on the picture of the phone to the left. You must decide which one. A number is not necessarily the same letter each time.

1. 9428 47 843 2472863373623 63 2
7867546 3484333 29 487 34263837?
7867546 74.

2. 9428 47 2 75353866'7 32867483
4678786368 86 7529? 87662663!

Answer Key

Word Search
From Page 5

```
J I R M O O N L I G H T C S J A
C M R W Y G O B L I N M R R M I
A L U A G S U H W S P E L L Q X
T D E A R R Z Z C V H C F Z E
X I E K F X C X W U K F F E L Y
Y S U P P M T G P L I K T K Q S
P O A U Y G W Y V C R F H W K T
V I L Q X B C E Q Q O N B H Y S
A N G B H F H E N N A K V G S S
R L R N Z W D X Y G F B O U O Q
W B O N I B A P C I U J M V T
I I R C M B T K N I F E X O S U
T R R Q S X S H R H Y T Y U H V
C G U R D U W X D Q H Q E L B
H Z H N N A G L O Z F G Q Y K E
I F W H A U N T E D P D P J L S
```

Cryptogram
From Page 6

1. Ahvatqcr uzn uc nplniincw ryhzin ys
   enwu-luzywncn, wxn aiucw aznlhzryz
   ys gqwuvqc U.

   Pumpkins are an excellent source of
   beta-carotene, the plant precursor of vitamin A.

2. Vmnb os usi xnee vhbxmdf bmnb ehtd
   bscdbmdz? Gzssk-knbdf!

   What do you call witches that live together?
   Broom-mates!

3. Akis yf cfe riuu i ahsrk skis uhlbg
   pc skb gbi? I gixyahsrk.

   What do you call a witch that lives by the sea?
   A sandwitch.

Alphabet Soup
From Page 7

```
Y G S K H A Z E L N U T L
R E W P C I S O N G G H Y
U R W O L Y Q W J H J B
H Q M V Y T H P I L L U P
H T P T R A D I T I O N G
Z Y E S T M G M S T E F
B N X Y S K U L L O L L
O I S G U I N G Q L J D
T O M B S T O N E C F U J
H B C A N D Y C O R N N J
W J N S L S F I D E R A P
B R S P O O L A N T E R N
W B G S C A H Y M S Y Q G
R M Q C L M G O B L I N F
U A S G M S X U A B F X F
Q E R V C M O M M Y X S E
H E M M D E A D L F H L F
V E S W W E B N R J U C F V
M P D I V I N A T I O N W
Q E T U C A T W E E N Y F
A H A U N T E D O A N G L
H W G O G N W E T C H S Z
R E C A R V E F W K H A
P U M K A N J O H M O O N
A O P E B E X I L E C E R
```

Dittos
From Page 8

Free Letter	Letter Bank
d	a b b c e g g h i i k l l l n o o o r t u v

1. b l a c k
2. b l o o d
3. n i g h t
4. d e v i l
5. g o u r d

Piece By Piece
From Page 9

what do you
call a skeleton
who won't
get a job?
lazy bones!

Word Scramble
From Page 10

1. CWHIT = WITCH
2. VRCEA = CARVE
3. MYUMM = MUMMY
4. TCA = CAT
5. LIAYDOH = HOLIDAY
6. ENMOD = DEMON
7. SEMCRA = SCREAM
8. UMMYM = MUMMY

Crypto Words
From Page 11

1. APLOH = BONES
2. FMWJ = DARK
3. FOYPL = DEMON
4. QPRCPL = POTION
5. GOMFHRPLO = HEADSTONE
6. GMELROF = HAUNTED
7. MLBOU = ANGEL
8. BWMNOXMWF = GRAVEYARD

Key Words
From Page 12

s k e l e t o n

1. g h o s t
2. m a k e u p
3. k n i f e
4. c h i l l
5. o r a n g e
6. n i g h t
7. b r o o m
8. t u r n i p

Two In
From Page 13

1. wit<u>c</u>hill

2. er<u>g</u>oblin

3. horr<u>o</u>range

4. ta<u>c</u>obweb

5. ghos<u>t</u>reet

Flip Phone Mania
From Page 14

1. 9428 47 2 32867483 33784628466 7768
   66 4255693362 5253 33743

   What is a favorite destination spot on
   Halloween? Lake Erie

2. 469 36 968 349 2 5225-6-52683762
   9484 2 7867546 72824!

   How do you fix a jack-o-lantern? With a pumpkin
   patch!

Interweave
From Page 15

1. aidsr <u>h</u>l l <u>b</u> a l n t s <u>d</u> a y

2. ealli r o o r <u>m</u> a l l

3. sttni b <u>a</u> z <u>l</u> h <u>a</u> t

4. srrei <u>j</u> <u>o</u> <u>c</u> k o l a n t <u>e</u> r n

5. egoar <u>j</u> h <u>o</u> <u>a</u> t a t u r i <u>e</u> s

Alphabet Soup
From Page 16

Bubble Words
From Page 17

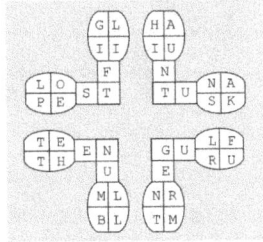

Piece By Piece
From Page 18

what is a
skeleton 's
favorite
instrument
to play? trombone !

Scramble
From Page 19

1. NIGTH =   NIGHT
2. RSMTOEN =   MONSTER
3. NHEWOLEAL =   HALLOWEEN
4. CARCDNNYO =   CANDYCORN
5. PLLSE =   SPELL
6. GORDU =   GOURD
7. ADUTHNE =   HAUNTED
8. RBWE =   BREW

Crypto Words
From Page 20

1. QGRMLNY =   PHANTOM
2. WRFI =   DARK
3. YDYYE =   MUMMY
4. HNFQKJ =   CORPSE
5. QDYQIVMURFY = PUMPKINFARM
6. SJZ =   WEB
7. GNTVWRE =   HOLIDAY
8. YRKI =   MASK

Key Words
From Page 21

t r a d i t i o n

1. t h r i l l
2. c i d e r
3. s c r e a m
4. d e v i l
5. s p i d e r
6. n i g h t
7. p o i s o n
8. t e r r o r
9. d e m o n

Two In
From Page 22

1. b e a n g e l
2. a c h e a d s t o n e
3. a m m o o n l i g h t
4. c h a p p l e
5. b a s h a d o w

Flip Phone Mania
From Page 23

1. 9428 47 843 2472863373623 63 2
   7867546 3484333 29 487 342638372
   7867546 74.

   What is the circumference of a pumpkin divided by its diameter? Pumpkin Pi.

2. 9428 47 2 75353866'7 32867483
   4678786368 86 75297 87662663!

   What is a skeleton's favorite instrument to play? TromBONE!

APPENDIX

Great Resources

BOOKS

Being Vegetarian for Dummies
Suzanne Havala, MS, RD (Cleveland, OH: IDG Books Worldwide, 2001)
Summary: This book provides an easy-to-understand look at vegetarian diets, including nutrition issues; practical tips, menu planning, and recipe modification; pregnancy; infants, children, and teens; and athletes.

How Not to Die
Michael Gregor, MD, and Gene Stone (New York: Flatiron Books, 2015)
Summary: Written by the physician behind the popular website Nutrition Facts, this book presents the scientific evidence behind the claims that a plant based can reverse and prevent many of the most common diseases plaguing us today.

Simply Vegan: Quick Vegetarian Meals, Third Edition
Debra Wasserman; nutrition section by Reed Mangels, PhD, RD (Baltimore, MD: the Vegetarian Resource Group, 1999)
Summary: This book features a nutrition section that briefly discusses key nutrients in the vegan diet. It also includes over 160 quick-and-easy recipes.

The Vegetarian Way: Total Health for You and Your Family
Virginia Messina, MPH, RD, and Mark Messina, PhD (New York: Crown Trade Paperbacks, 1996)
Summary: This authoritative and comprehensive handbook provides information on all aspects of vegetarian nutrition, including nutrient sources and nutritional needs for vegetarians of all ages. Includes recipes, menus, food guides, and cooking tips.

Vegan for Life
Jack Norris and Virginia Messina (Boston, MA: Da Capo Press, 2011)
Summary: This outstanding guide to vegan diets thoroughly covers basic nutrition topics for vegans, provides a vegan food guide; addresses the needs of children and pregnant women; and discusses topics like being overweight, eating disorders, and vegan athletes.

Vegan & Vegetarian FAQ: Answers to Your Frequently Asked Questions
Davida Gypsy Breier; nutrition section by Reed Mangels, PhD, RD (Baltimore, MD: the Vegetarian Resource Group, 2001)

Summary: This book provides hundreds of answers on everything from food ingredients to vegetarian nutrition to vegetarian cooking.

MAGAZINES, NEWSLETTERS, & PAMPHLETS

"Position of the American Dietetic Association: Vegetarian Diets"
American Dietetic Association (ADA)
PDF: https://www.eatrightpro.org/~/media/eatrightpro%20files/practice/position%20and%20practice%20papers/position%20papers/vegetarian-diet.ashx
Summary: The American Dietetic Association's position paper on vegetarian nutrition. This technical paper includes nutrients of consideration for those on vegetarian diets, therapeutic uses of a vegetarian diet, and environmental concerns attached to the diet.

"Vegetarianism in a Nutshell"; "Veganism in a Nutshell"
The Vegetarian Resource Group
Web versions: www.vrg.org/nutshell/nutshell.htm; www.vrg.org/nutshell/vegan.htm
Summary: These pamphlets contain basic information on vegetarian and vegan nutrition and foods.

Vegetarians in Paradise
Website: www.vegparadise.com
Summary: A vegan web magazine providing information on types of vegetarians, getting started in vegetarianism, foods, protein sources, and benefits of vegetarianism.

Vegetarian Journal
Website: www.vrg.org/journal (includes selected articles from previous issues and subscription information)
Summary: This quarterly magazine is published by the Vegetarian Resource Group. It includes practical tips for vegetarian meal planning, articles relevant to vegetarian nutrition, recipes, and natural-food-product reviews.

WEBSITES

NutritionFacts.org
Michael Gregor, MD
Website: www.nutritionfacts.org
Summary: Created by a plant based physician, this website features videos and blog posts breaking down the latest in health nutrition research in a useful and easy to understand way.

Evidence-Based Nutrient Recommendations
A project of Vegan Outreach

Website: www.veganhealth.org
Summary: Well-referenced collection of nutrition information for vegans. Includes information on health benefits, meal planning ideas, and nutritional issues of which vegans should be aware, focusing on recommended daily intakes of important nutrients.

Health & Nutrition
The Vegetarian Society of the United Kingdom
Website: www.vegsoc.org/health
Summary: This site includes a very complete listing of resources and fact sheets on many aspects of vegetarian nutrition, including basic nutrition, protein, fats and cholesterol, calcium, iron, vitamin B 12 , and zinc.

Health & Nutrition
The Physicians Committee for Responsible Medicine
Website: www.pcrm.org/health
Summary: Resources, research, and recipes developed by plant based physicians.

Vegan Outreach
Website: www.veganoutreach.org
Summary: The website of a grassroots vegan advocacy group offering advice on how to make the vegan transition.

The Vegan RD
Virginia Messina, MPH, RD
Website: www.theveganrd.com
Summary: Well-researched responses to questions about all aspects of vegetarian nutrition and foods. Updated weekly.

Vegetarian Resource Group
Website: www.vrg.org
Summary: This website contains a wealth of information on vegetarian nutrition—including nutrients like iron, calcium, protein, and vitamin B 12 —as well as reprints of nutrition-related articles from Vegetarian Journal.

Vegetarian Nutrition
Food and Nutrition Information Center, USDA
Website: https://www.nal.usda.gov/fnic/vegetarian-nutrition
Summary: Links to web resources on many aspects of vegetarianism.

Vegetarian Nutrition
A dietetic practice group of the Academy of Nutrition and Dietetics

Website: www.vegetariannutrition.net
Summary: Tools from evidence-based research for planning all types of vegetarian meals.

HappyCow
Website: www.happycow.net
Summary: An online service that lists restaurants in your area catering to vegan and vegetarian diets. Also has a downloadable phone app.

One Green Planet
Website: www.onegreenplanet.org
Summary: An independent publishing platform dedicated to bringing info about sustainable living, animal welfare issues, compassionate living, and providing vegan recipes.

Isa Chandra
Website: www.isachandra.com
Summary: Plant based recipes from restaurant owner and cookbook author Isa Chandra.

Oh She Glows
Website: www.ohsheglows.com
Summary: Award-winning recipe blog featuring healthy plant based recipes, mostly gluten free.

SOCIAL MEDIA

Imperfectly Vegan www.facebook.com/imperfectlyvegan/; www.instagram.com/imperfectlyvegan_/
Sacred Exploration www.facebook.com/sacredexploration/
NutritionFacts.org www.facebook.com/NutritionFacts.org/
Plant-Based Dietician www.facebook.com/PlantBasedDietitian/
The Vegan RD www.facebook.com/TheVeganRD/
Direct Action Everywhere www.facebook.com/directactioneverywhere/
Mercy For Animals www.facebook.com/mercyforanimals/

COOKBOOKS

Cooking Vegetarian
Vesanto Mellina and Joseph Forest (Toronto: Macmillan, 1996)

Everyday Cooking with Dr. Dean Ornish: 150 Easy, Low-Fat, High-Flavor Recipes
Dean Ornish, MD (New York: HarperCollins, 1997)

Forks over Knives—the Cookbook: Over 300 Recipes for Plant-Based Eating All Through the Year
Del Sroufe, Julieanna Hever, Isa Chandra Moskowitz, and Darshana Thacker (2012)

Joy of Cooking: All About Vegetarian Cooking
Irma S. Rombauer, Marion Rombauer Becker, Ethan Becker (New York: Scribner, 2000)

Lorna Sass' Complete Vegetarian Kitchen: Where Good Flavors and Good Health Meet
Lorna Sass (New York: William Morrow & Co., 2002)

Madhur Jaffrey's World Vegetarian
Madhur Jaffrey (New York: Random House, 2002).

Meatless Meals for Working People: Quick and Easy Vegetarian Recipes, Fourth Edition
Debra Wasserman and Charles Stahler (Baltimore, MD: the Vegetarian Resource Group, 2004)

Moosewood Restaurant New Classics
Moosewood Collective (New York: Clarkson Potter, 2001).

More Soy of Cooking: Healthful Renditions of Classic Traditional Meals
Marie Oser (New York: John Wiley & Sons, 2000)

Soy Desserts: 101 Fun and Fabulously Healthy Recipes
Patricia Greenberg (New York: Regan Books, 2000)

The Complete Soy Cookbook
Paulette Mitchell (New York: Macmillan, 1998)

The Gluten-Free Vegan
Susan O'Brien (Philadelphia: Da Capo Press, 2007)

The How Not To Die Cookbook
Michael Gregor (London: Pan Macmillan U.K, 2017)

The Kind Diet
Alicia Silverstone (Emmaus, PA: Rodale Books, 2011)

The New Moosewood Cookbook
Mollie Katzen (Berkeley, CA: Ten Speed Press, 2000)

The Sacred Art of Eating: Healing Our Relationship with Food
Lisa Tremont Ota (CreateSpace Independent Publishing Platform, 2016)

The Vegetarian 5-Ingredient Gourmet
Nava Atlas (New York: Broadway Books, 2001)

The Vegetarian Gourmet's Easy International Recipes
Bobbie Hinman (Chicago: Surrey Books, 2001)

Vegan Meals for One or Two
Nancy Berkoff, RD (Baltimore, MD: the Vegetarian Resource Group, 2001)

Vegetarian Cooking for Dummies
Suzanne Havala, MS, RD (New York: Hungry Minds, 2001)

FOOD SECURITY RESOURCES

Food Not Bombs provides meals and groceries to thousands who need it, free of charge, at various locations around the United States, using food donated to them by grocery stores, bakeries, and produce markets (www.foodnotbombs.net).

The US Department of Agriculture's Food and Nutrition Service administers a range of nutrition assistance programs throughout the United States (www.fns.usda.gov/programs-and-services).

The Food Research and Action Center, a national nonprofit organization, is working to improve public policies and public-private partnerships to eradicate hunger and undernutrition in the United States (www.frac.org).

The United Nations' World Food Programme includes among its missions saving lives during refugee crises improving the nutrition and quality of life of the world's most vulnerable people, and enabling development (www.wfp.org).

The International Food Policy Research Institute provides policy solutions that reduce hunger and malnutrition throughout the world order (www.ifpri.org).

BAKING CONVERSIONS

Quickly scale up or down recipes using this handy chart!

Tsp	Tbsp	Cup	Fluid Oz
3	1	1/16	1/2
6	2	1/8	1
12	4	1/4	2
18	6	3/8	3
24	8	1/2	4
36	12	3/4	6
64	16	1	8

2 cups = 1 pint   4 cups = 1 quart   4 quarts = 1 gallon

Want more great ideas about a vegan lifestyle and even how to hold a vegan dinner party?
Check out The Sacred Art of Eating

Want to join a like-minded people going vegan and share support and ideas?
Join the Imperfectly Vegan Facebook group.

Follow me on Twitter for great tips, recipes and more.

NOT SO SCARY EGG REPLACEMENTS

Use these instead of eggs in the non-vegan recipes you already have!

= 1 Egg	Works Best For
1/4 cup applesauce, or other fruit puree	Quick breads, muffins, cakes
1/2 mashed banana	Quick breads, muffins, pancakes, brownies, cookies - adds sweetness & some banana flavor
1/4 cup silken tofu	Cakes or other moist recipes - it can be heavy
1/4 cup soy yogurt	Quick breads, muffins, cakes
1 tbsp ground flaxseed or chia seeds + 3 tbsp water; let sit for 5 minutes	Recipes that call for vinegar or baking powder/soda
Aquafaba (liquid from 1 can of unsalted chickpeas)	Meringues, macarons, mousse
1 tsp baking powder + 1 tbsp apple cider vinegar, mixed & added immediately	Quick breads, muffins, cakes
1 tsp baking powder + 1 tbsp vegetable oil + 2 tbsp water	Gluten free baking
1 tsp agar powder dissolved in 1 tbsp water	Replacement for recipes that use egg whites
Commercial egg replacement; follow directions	Versatile in baked goods

PARTY PREPARATIONS LIST

Date/Time: _____

Event type: BRUNCH

Checklist:

☐ Water and cups with Halloween stickers (so that each person can personalize their own cup)

☐ Halloween music

☐ Food signs placed

☐ Napkins and plates

☐ Forks __ Knives __ Spoons__

☐ Cups (smoothie, hot cider, coffee, tea)

☐ Game supplies

    ☐ Bobbing for Apples

        ☐ Tub or basin

        ☐ Apples (a variety of color and taste is extra fun)

    ☐ Spider Web Toss

        ☐ Ball of white yarn

    ☐ Mummy Wrap Contest

        ☐ Toilet paper

        ☐ Masking tape

    ☐ 19 Halloween Puzzles

        ☐ Printed puzzles (black print on orange paper is fun)

        ☐ Pens

☐ Trick-or-Treat Bags (optional)

Food:

Coffee (regular)	("Jugular coffee")	Green Tea	("WITCH's Green Tea")
Coffee (decaffeinated)	("DECAPITATED coffee")	Apple Cider	("Hot Apple SPIDER")
Soy or coconut creamer	("SCREAM")		
Sugar			

As well as any ingredients from your selection of Recipes for a Tasty Transformation.

Ready to Print Party Food Signs

Below are fun food signs that are all ready to print and cut out. I recommend you use card stock so they have a bit of substance to them, though plain paper will work, too. Cut on the solid line, and fold along the dotted one, as shown in the first sample, so that you can stand these signs up. Or, instead of folding them, you can stand a single sheet sideways in a placeholder. Or, here are some free sites to help you make these food identifiers (or name cards) more formal:

• http://www.seatingcard.com/
• https://www.placecard.me/
• On Canva: https://www.canva.com/create/place-cards/
• On MS Word: http://smallbusiness.chron.com/make-place-cards-microsoft-word-53913.html

Cut on this line

_____

Fold here

- -

DECAPITATED COFFEE

_____

Cut on this line
_____

Fold Here
- -

JUGULAR COFFEE
_____

Cut on this line
_____

Fold Here
- -

COCONUT SCREAM
_____

Cut on this line
_____

Fold Here
- -

WITCH'S BREW
_____

Imperfectly Vegan™: Halloween Style

Cut on this line

Fold Here
- -

PUMPKIN SMOOTHIE

Cut on this line

Fold Here
- -

GOBLIN EYES

Cut on this line

Fold Here
- -

VAMPIRE BITES

Cut on this line

Fold Here

VAMPIRE BLOOD

Cut on this line

Fold Here

CADAVERloupe

Cut on this line

Fold Here

BOO-BERRIES

Imperfectly Vegan™: Halloween Style

Cut on this line
_____

Fold Here
- -

BOO-NANA BREAD

_____

Cut on this line
_____

Fold Here
- -

HARVEST SOUP

_____

Cut on this line
_____

Fold Here
- -

NOT-DEAD BREAD

_____

Cut on this line

Fold Here

HOT APPLE SPIDER

Cut on this line

Fold Here

PUMPKIN ALE

Cut on this line

Fold Here

ROASTED TOMATO DRIP

Imperfectly Vegan™: Halloween Style

Cut on this line

Fold Here

BOO-GELS + SCREAM CHEESE

Cut on this line

Fold Here

SCREAMY CHOCOLATE MOUSSE

Cut on this line

Fold Here

BAT BRAINS

Cut on this line

_____

Fold Here

- -

DARK AS NIGHT BROWNIES

_____

Cut on this line

_____

Fold Here

- -

CRACKERS

_____

Cut on this line

_____

Fold Here

- -

WATER

_____

Imperfectly Vegan™: Halloween Style

Cut on this line

Fold Here

SPOOKY COOKIES

Cut on this line

Fold Here

EYEBALL PUNCH

Cut on this line

Fold Here

PUMPKIN PIE PANCAKES

ABOUT THE AUTHORS

Lisa Tremont Ota's passion about the unbreakable links between health and spirituality is the result of over 30 years of academic, professional, and personal exploration. A registered dietitian nutritionist (UC Berkeley, 1987) with advanced degrees in public health (UC Berkeley, 1990) and spirituality (Holy Names College, 1996), Lisa is uniquely qualified to help us heal and nourish our relationship with food.

How did deciding between types of grain lead people to stand paralyzed in the cereal aisle of their local grocery store?

How has making choices about what to eat evolve into a nation obsessed with one fad diet after another?

How is it possible that so many people don't have enough to eat when the planet serves up enough for everyone?

These are the questions that kept Lisa up at night, and which led her to pursue a career in nutrition and dietetics. She has developed wellness programs for non-profit organizations, governmental agencies, and corporations, including Safeway, Pacific Bell, and Barbara's Bakery. She directed the first statewide distribution of UC Berkeley's The Wellness Guide to over one million English- and Spanish-speaking participants in California's Women, Infants, and Children (WIC) Program. Over the years, she has led over 100 grocery store tours, including one with Dr. Nancy Snyderman for KPIX Channel 5 News, has made appearances on KGO TV's The View from the Bay, and has provided hundreds of customized presentations to a wide variety of audiences. Venues include SF VegFest, SF Wellness Central, and VegCurious. Lisa is also an enthusiastic representative of The JuicePlus+ Company.

Serving up a much more expansive view of what it means to eat, Lisa is the author of The Sacred Art of Eating. This book and her ImperfectlyVegan™ brand highlight our relationship with food as a spiritual path that is both exciting and necessary for individual well-being and planetary sustainability. With an inclusive approach based on public health strategies, The Sacred Art of Eating catalyzes desperately needed conversation and behavior change toward true integrity of body, mind, and spirit.

Following the book's metaphorical dinner party, Lisa hosts unique ImperfectlyVegan™ dining experiences which provide a delicious and entertaining format in which to practice the book's messages.

Lisa is thrilled to be mother of two adult children whom she homeschooled for six years. She is a proud native of the San Francisco Bay Area and considers the planet to be her home. When not cooking, gardening, hiking, or traveling, you'll likely find her on the dance floor.

Reilly Gardine holds a Bachelor's degree in Nutritional Sciences from UC Berkeley, and is a certified personal trainer and social justice activist. Their experiences with poor health growing up led them to a plant based lifestyle, as well as a drive to study nutrition and health so that they could help others struggling with a decreased quality of life due to sub-optimal health. This soon morphed into a strong desire for justice for those who lack the ability to fight for themselves, as delving into vegan nutrition can unsurprisingly lead one to uncover the inherent atrocities of an industry that profits off of animal suffering. A vegetarian for over thirteen years, and vegan for over seven, Reilly has multiple years of experience in animal rights organizing, advocating against the oppression of animals in all realms of animal exploitation through campaigns, outreach, international conference organizing, and more. Combining the need for animal liberation with whole foods plant-based nutrition came easy for them - after all, it makes sense to want to dismantle the industry that tortures billions a year while sending millions to the hospital. As an ImperfectlyVegan™ team member, they have been able to do just that - mix their compassion for animals with their interest in human health and nutrition.

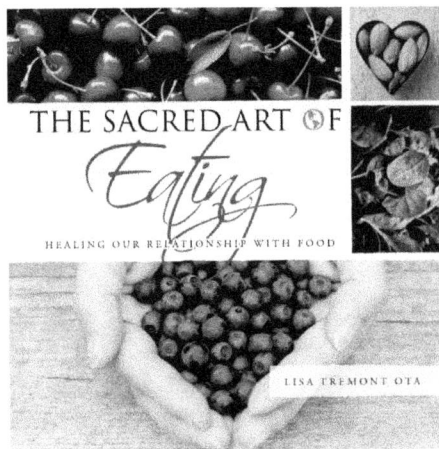

THE SACRED ART OF
Eating

HEALING OUR RELATIONSHIP WITH FOOD

LISA TREMONT OTA

Want more wisdom about how to heal our relationship with food? **Get The Sacred Art of Eating Book.**

Join us here to get current information and support: ImperfectlyVegan™ Facebook Group.

Keep up with upcoming events, meet like-minded people and begin your own personal transformation to better health and increased integrity!

www.ingramcontent.com/pod-product-compliance
Lightning Source LLC
Chambersburg PA
CBHW081543040426
42448CB00015B/3204